Herbert Baxter Adams

Maryland's Influence in Founding a National Commonwealth

Or, the History of the Accession of Public Lands by the Old Confederation

Herbert Baxter Adams

Maryland's Influence in Founding a National Commonwealth
Or, the History of the Accession of Public Lands by the Old Confederation

ISBN/EAN: 9783337062651

Printed in Europe, USA, Canada, Australia, Japan

Cover: Foto ©Suzi / pixelio.de

More available books at **www.hansebooks.com**

Fund-Publication, No. 11.

MARYLAND'S

INFLUENCE IN FOUNDING A

National Commonwealth.

OR THE

History of the Accession of Public Lands

BY THE OLD CONFEDERATION.

A Paper read before the Maryland Historical Society.

April 9, 1877.

BY

HERBERT B. ADAMS, PH. D.,

FELLOW IN HISTORY, JOHNS HOPKINS UNIVERSITY.

Baltimore, 1877.

"The vacant lands are a favorite object to Maryland."

MADISON,
On the plan for a general revenue, 1783.

"There is nothing which binds one country or one State to another but interest."

WASHINGTON,
On the Potomac Scheme for Opening a Channel of Trade between East and West, 1785.

"There is no truth more thoroughly established, than that there exists in the economy and course of nature an indissoluble union between virtue and happiness, between duty and advantage, between the genuine maxims of an honest and magnanimous policy, and the solid rewards of public prosperity and felicity."

WASHINGTON,
Inaugural Address, 1789.

PRINTED BY JOHN MURPHY,
PRINTER TO THE MARYLAND HISTORICAL SOCIETY,
BALTIMORE, 1877.

MARYLAND'S INFLUENCE

IN

Founding a National Commonwealth.

THE claims of England to the lands immediately west of the Alleghany mountains and to the region north-west of the Ohio river, were successfully vindicated in the French and Indian War. By the treaty of Paris, in 1763, the English became the acknowledged masters, not only of the disputed lands back of their settlements, but of Canada and of the entire Western country as far as the Mississippi river. This was the first curtailment of Louisiana, that vast inland region, over which France had extended her claims by virtue of explorations from Canada to the Gulf of Mexico. Although now restricted by the treaty of Paris to the comparatively unknown territory beyond the Mississippi, Louisiana was destined to undergo still further diminution, and, like Virginia, which was once a geographical term for half a continent, to become finally a state of definite limits and historic character. Ceded by

France to Spain, at the close of the above-mentioned war, in compensation for losses sustained by the latter in aiding France against England, and ceded back again to France in 1800, through the influence of Napoleon, these lands beyond the Mississippi were purchased by our Government of the First Consul in 1803, and out of the southeastern portion of the so-called "Louisiana Purchase," that State[1] was created, in 1812, which perpetuates the name of Louis XIV., as Virginia does the fame of a virgin queen.

But it is not with Louisiana or the Louisiana Purchase that we are especially concerned in this paper. We have to do with a still earlier accession of national territory, with those lands which were separated from French dominion by conquest and by the treaty of Paris, and, more especially, with that triangular region east of the Mississippi, south of the Great Lakes, and north-west of the Ohio, for here, as we shall see, was established the first territorial commonwealth of the old Confederation, and that too through the effective influence and far-sighted policy of Maryland

---

[1] The final outcome of French dominion in this country is Louisiana, with its French inheritance of Roman Law. Having passed of late years through many corrupt phases of prætorian, proconsular, and dictatorial government, it was perhaps an historic necessity that she should revive the Roman theory of sovereignty, as did Louis XIV., by the aid of his court-lawyers, and reässert *la puissance souveraine d'une république* and *l'état c'est moi*, in the form of an enlightened absolutism of its sovereign people.

in opposing the grasping land claims of Virginia and three of the Northern States. The history of the accession of those public lands which are best known to Americans as the North-west Territory, and the constitutional importance of that accession as a basis of permanent union for thirteen loosely confederated States, and as a field for republican expansion under the sovereign control of Congress, may be presented under three general heads:

1. The land claims of Virginia, Massachusetts, Connecticut, and New York.
2. The influence of Maryland in securing a general cession of western territory for the public good.
3. The origin of our territorial government and the true basis of national sovereignty.

I. THE LAND CLAIMS.

Having indicated the historic place and territorial situation of the western lands in question, we shall now turn to the specific claims of Virginia, Massachusetts, Connecticut, and New York, the only States, which after the separation of the colonies from the mother country, had any legal title to lands north-west of the Ohio.

The charter granted by James I. to South Virginia, in 1609, was the most comprehensive of all the colonial charters, for it embraced the entire north-west and, within certain limits, all the islands along the coast of the South Sea. It is not very surprising that the ideas and language of the privy council should have been somewhat hazy as to the exact whereabouts of the South Sea, for Stith,[1] one of the early historians of Virginia, tells us that in 1608, when the London Company were soliciting their patent, an expedition was organized under Captain Newport to sail up the James river and find a passage to the South Sea. Captain John Smith also was once commissioned to seek a new route to China by ascending the Chickahominy! This charter of 1609 is the only one which we shall cite in this paper, for it was especially against the enormous claims of Virginia that Maryland raised so just and effective a protest. The following is the grant:

"All those lands, countries and territories situate, lying and being in that part of America called Virginia, from the point of land called Cape or Point Comfort, all along the sea-coast to the northward two hundred miles and from the said Point or Cape Comfort, all along the sea-coast to the southward two hundred miles; and all that space and circuit of land lying from the sea-coast of the precinct aforesaid, up into the land throughout,

---

[1] Stith's History of the first discovery and settlement of Virginia. Reprinted for Joseph Sabin, 1865, p. 77.

from sea to sea, west and north-west; and also all the islands lying within one hundred miles along the coast of both seas of the precinct aforesaid."[1]

The extraordinary ambiguity of this grant of 1609, which was always appealed to as a legal title by Virginia, was first shown by Thomas Paine, the great publicist of the American and French Revolutions, in a pamphlet called "Public Good,"[2] written in 1780, and containing, as the author says upon his title page, "an investigation of the claims of Virginia to the vacant western territory, and of the right of the United States to the same; with some outlines of a plan for laying out a new State, to be applied as a fund, for carrying on the war, or redeeming the national debt." Paine shows how the words of the charter of 1609 could be interpreted in different ways; for example, the words "all along the sea-coast" might signify a straight line or the indented line of the coast. The chief ambiguity, however, lay in the interpretation of the words "up into the land throughout, from sea to sea, west and north-west." From which point was the north-west line to be drawn, from the point on the sea-coast two hundred miles above, or from the point two hundred miles below

---

[1] Laws of the United States respecting the Public Lands, (Washington, 1828.) p. 81.
[2] Works of Thomas Paine, I., p. 267.

Cape Comfort? The charter does not state distinctly. The logical order of terms would imply that the lower point below Cape Comfort, should be taken as the starting point for the northwestern line. In that case, Virginia would have a triangular boundary and a definite area something larger than Pennsylvania.

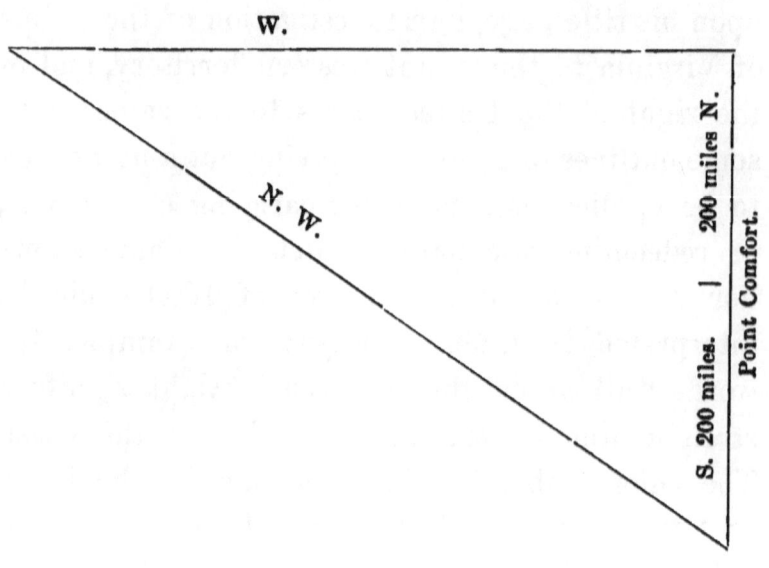

The more favorable interpretation for Virginia and, perhaps, in view of the expression "from sea to sea," more natural interpretation, was to draw the north-western line from the point on the sea-coast two hundred miles above Point Comfort and the western line from the southern limit below Point Comfort. This gave Virginia the greater part, at least, of the entire north-west, for the lines diverged continually.

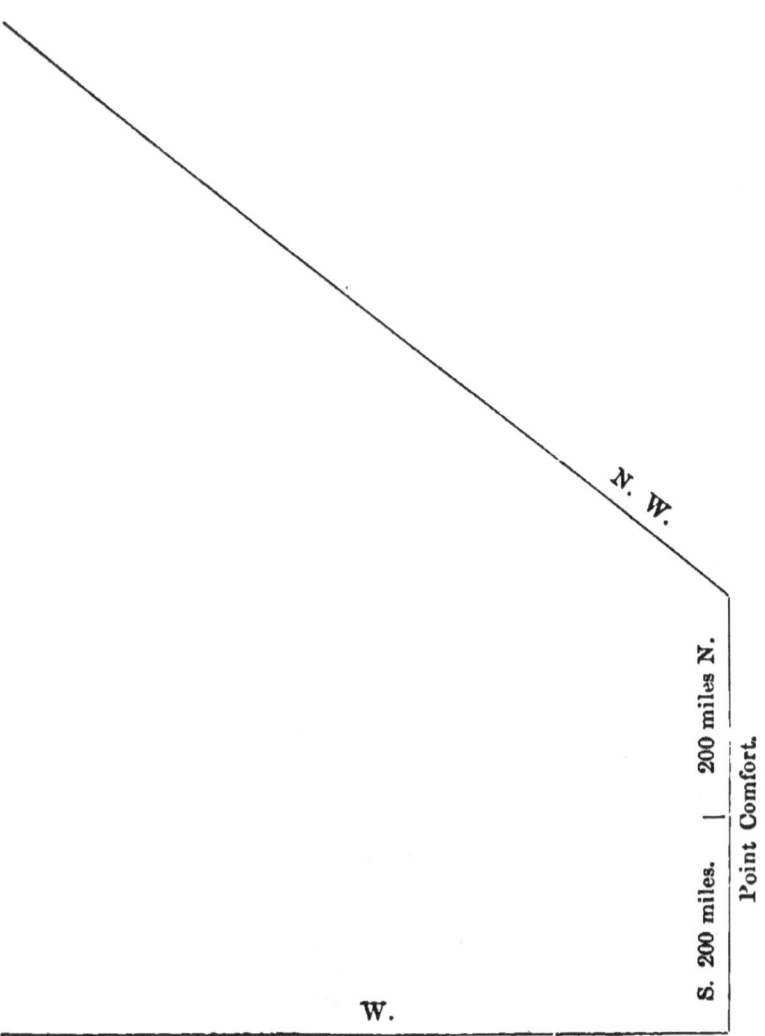

In 1624, the London Company was dissolved, and Virginia became a royal province, the Governor being appointed by the King, but the people electing a House of Burgesses. No alteration appears to have been made at that time in the boundaries established by the charter of 1609, but the northern limits of Virginia were afterwards curtailed by grants to Lord Baltimore and William Penn, and the southern limits by a grant to the proprietors of Carolina.[1] From a letter of Edmund Burke to the General Assembly of New York, for which province he was employed as agent, it is clear that, in questions concerning the boundary of royal provinces, it was the uniform doctrine and practice of the Lords Commissioners for Trade and Plantations, to regard "no rule but the king's will."[2] A royal proclamation was issued in 1763, prohibiting colonial governors from granting patents for land beyond the sources of any of the rivers which flow into the Atlantic ocean from the west or north-

---

[1] The charter of Maryland was granted in 1632, and may be found in Bacon's Laws of Maryland at Large, or in Hazard 1., pp. 327-36. The charter of Pennsylvania bears the date of 1661, and is contained in Proud's History of Pennsylvania, I., pp. 171-87. The original charter of Carolina, (1663,) for which Locke's famous constitution was written, is said to have been copied from the charter of Maryland. See Lucas' Charters of the Old English Colonies, London, 1850, p. 97.

[2] Burke's letter, which is most interesting for its exposition of the Quebec Bill of 1774, annexing to Canada the country north-west of the Ohio, was first published in the New York Historical Society Collections, 2d Series, II., pp. 219-25.

west.¹ Washington regarded this proclamation as a temporary expedient for quieting the minds of the Indians, and he proceeded therefore, with the greatest tranquillity, to seek out and survey good lands for future speculation.²

But efforts were being made to establish a new colony back of Virginia. The so-called "Ohio Company" had been founded as early as 1748, by Thomas Lee, Lawrence Washington, Augustine Washington and others, for the colonization of the western country.³ A grant had been obtained, from the crown, of five hundred thousand acres of land in the region of the Ohio, and the efforts of this company to open up a road into the western valleys precipitated the French and Indian war. Probably the proclamation of 1763 was partly designed to pacify the Indians by reserving for their use, under the sovereign protection of England, the lands back of the Alleghanies and beyond the Ohio, but schemes for a new government in that region were being discussed in England as well as in America.⁴

In 1766, Benjamin Franklin⁵ was laying plans for a second great land company, which was

---

1 This proclamation is to be found in the Land Laws of the United States, pp. 84–88 or in Franklin's Works, IV., p. 374, at the conclusion of his famous paper on "Ohio Settlement."
2 See letter to Crawford, September 21, 1767. Sparks' Life and Writings of Washington, II ; p. 346.
3 Sparks' Life and Writings of Washington. II., p. 479.
4 A pamphlet was published in London, in 1763, entitled "The Advantages of a settlement upon the Ohio in North America"
5 Works of Franklin, IV., p. 233.

finally organized and called the Vandalia or Walpole Company. It was composed of thirty-two Americans and two Londoners. Benjamin Franklin was really the moving spirit in the enterprise, but he persuaded Thomas Walpole, a London banker of eminence, to serve as the figure-head. The company petitioned, in 1769, for a grant of two and a half million acres of western land lying between the thirty-eighth and forty-second parallels of latitude and to the east of the river Scioto. Franklin was in London and labored hard with Cabinet officers and the Board of Trade for the success of Walpole's petition. It was urged that the company offered more for this grant than the whole region back of the mountains had cost the British Government, at the Treaty of Fort Stanwix with the Indians, in 1768. The claims of the Ohio Company were also merged in this new scheme, but the report thereon was long delayed through the influence of Lord Hillsborough. A "new colony back of Virginia" was much talked of, however, about the year 1770. Lord Hillsborough himself had some correspondence that year with the Governor of Virginia on this subject.[1] From a letter of George Washington to Lord Botetourt, and from subsequent correspondence between Washington and Lord Dunmore, Botetourt's successor as Governor of Virginia, it

[1] See Works of Thomas Paine, I., 290.

is perfectly clear that a new and independent colony was in prospect back of the Alleghanies.[1]

Indeed, a rival scheme, under the name of the Mississippi Company, seems to have been organized by gentlemen of Virginia, among whom Francis Lightfoot Lee, Richard Henry Lee, Arthur Lee, and George Washington were conspicuous, but their petition, in 1769, for two and a half million acres of back land was never heard from after it had been referred to the Board of Trade.[2] Walpole's petition, however, after a delay of three years, was, through the influence of Lord Hillsborough, unfavorably reported. Franklin immediately prepared an answer, which is said to be "one of the ablest tracts he ever penned,"[3] and in which he so utterly refuted the arguments of Lord Hillsborough that Walpole's petition was finally granted by the Crown, August 14, 1772. Lord Hillsborough was so mortified that he resigned his position as Cabinet Minister and President of the Board of Trade.

In the Washington-Crawford correspondence, from 1772 to 1774, there are several allusions to the prospect of a "new government on the Ohio."[4]

---

[1] Writings of Washington, II., pp. 356, 360.
[2] See Plain Facts, Philadelphia, 1781, p. 69.
[3] Sparks' Life and Writings of Washington, II., p. 485. Franklin's paper, which is entitled "Ohio Settlement," may be found in his Works, IV., pp. 324–374.
[4] The Washington-Crawford Letters concerning Western Lands. Edited by C. W. Butterfield, (Cincinnati, Robert Clarke & Co., 1877,) pp. 25, 30, 35.

Washington, in a letter dated September 25, 1773, desires to secure ten thousand acres of land as near as possible to "the western bounds of the new colony,"[1] that is, just beyond the Scioto, and, in a Baltimore newspaper of that year, he advertises for sale twenty thousand acres of land on the Great Kanawha and Ohio rivers, observing that "if the scheme for establishing a new government on the Ohio, in the manner talked of, should ever be effected, these must be among the most valuable lands in it."[2] It was confidently expected, after the treaty between the Crown of Great Britain and the Indians, in 1768, at Fort Stanwix, that the lines of the colonies would be reëxtended beyond the Alleghany mountains, or, in other words, that the limits imposed by the royal proclamation of 1763 would fall, but there is no evidence that this expectation was ever realized by any act of the King in council. It was rumored, indeed, at various times after Walpole's Grant had been secured, that "the new government on the Ohio" had fallen through and that Virginia was authorized to reässert her ancient charter boundaries, but these rumors appear to have been false. The legal title of the Walpole

[1] Washington-Crawford Letters, p. 30. See also Washington's letter to Dunmore, November 2, 1773. Washington's Writings, II., p. 378.
[2] Maryland Journal and the Baltimore Advertiser, August 20, 1773. A fac-simile of this number was reprinted last year (1875) by the Baltimore American.

Company was not, indeed, fully perfected when revolutionary troubles broke out, but it is evident from a report in the Journals of Congress on the claims of this company, generally known as the Vandalia, that the King and council had really agreed to erect the region back of Virginia into a separate colony, and that the agreement was completed all but affixing the seals and passing certain forms of office. While it was held, in the above report, that the allowance to a single company of such immense land claims, was incompatible with the interests and policy of the United States, it was recommended that the American members of the Vandalia be reimbursed by Congress in distinct and separate land grants, for their share in the purchase of the above tract.[1]

The consideration with which the claims of the Vandalia are treated in this report, which dismisses so summarily the pretensions of the Illinois and Wabash Companies, shows conclusively that there was some essence of right and legality in the original Walpole grant. At all events, it was recognized before the Revolution as taking the precedence of Virginia's claim to jurisdiction over the lands west of the Alleghanies. Lord Dunmore, in the summer of 1773, promised Washington's land agent to grant certain patents on the Ohio

[1] Journals of Congress, IV., p. 23.

in case the new government did not take place,[1] and in the fall of that year he wrote to Washington in the most positive terms: "I do not mean to grant any patents on the western waters, as I do not think I am at present empowered so to do."[2] Lord Dunmore had, however, at some previous date, issued patents to Washington for above twenty thousand acres of land on the Great Kanawha and Ohio rivers, as we know from the latter's advertisement, above mentioned, in the Maryland Journal and Baltimore Advertiser of August 20, 1773. The Governor of Virginia had no jurisdiction outside of his own province, but he had the right to grant from the King's domain two hundred thousand acres, in bounty-lands, to officers and soldiers who had served in the French and Indian war, and who should personally apply to him for land-warrants: To every field officer, five thousand acres; to every captain, three thousand; to every subaltern or staff officer, two hundred; and to every private soldier, fifty acres. These grants could be made in Canada or Florida, or in the so-called "Crown lands." The latter term was usually applied, after the proclamation of 1763, to the lands back of the Alleghanies and beyond the Ohio.

Private surveys in the above region had begun long before the time of Walpole's Grant, and the

---

[1] Washington-Crawford Letters, p. 35.
[2] Writings of Washington, II., p. 379.

claims of officers and soldiers had, to some extent, been bought up by speculators. Washington and his land agent, William Crawford, had been particularly active in seeking out good tracts of land in the western country. As a field officer, Washington was entitled, under the proclamation, to five thousand acres of bounty-land, but there is positive evidence to show that he had surveys for over seventy thousand acres; that he secured patents, in the names of officers and soldiers, for over sixty thousand, and that he himself was the owner of, at least, thirty-two thousand acres, which he called "the cream of the country—the first choice of it." There is a charming frankness in Washington's statement to the Reverend John Witherspoon concerning these lands. "It is not reasonable to suppose," he says, "that those who had the first choice, [who] had five years allowed them to make it in and a large district to survey in, were inattentive to the quality of the soil or the advantages of the situation."[1] There was nothing discreditable to Washington in his land speculations. We can only admire that far-sighted wisdom which so early discerned the importance of the western country, and that practical sagacity which was as great in affairs of private enterprise

---

[1] Washington-Crawford Letters, p. 78. A strong light is thrown upon Washington's character by this correspondence, but strong natures, like his, bear strong light. For documentary evidence on the subject of Washington's Land Speculations, see Appendix.

as it was afterwards in the affairs of state. It is certain, moreover, that in his business undertakings, Washington contemplated "an extensive public benefit as well as private advantage,"[1] for already before the Revolution, he had begun a correspondence relative to the importation of Germans from the Palatinate to colonize his lands.[2] Washington is the prototype of that public spirit and private enterprise which are so characteristic of Americans, and which, after all, constitute the life-principle of the American Republic. While investigating the nature of those material interests out of which the American Union was developed, it is not improper to glance thus, in passing, at the worldly characteristics of the Father of his Country. This question of land-claims is so interwoven with land-grants and land-speculations, both private and public, that it is necessary, for a proper understanding of the subject, to trace out, here and there, lines of individual conduct and the threads of personal motive.

It is uncertain when Lord Dunmore[3] first began to issue patents for the bounty-lands. We know that he must have patented upwards of twenty

---

[1] See letter to Crawford about the Salt Springs, Washington-Crawford Letters, p. 31, or Appendix to this paper.
[2] See Writings of Washington, II., pp 382–7.
[3] That Lord Dunmore patented Washington's land is evident from the latter's own statements. See Washington-Crawford Letters, p. 77. For the relation between Lord Dunmore and Washington, and for the former's interest in looking over the ground before granting further patents, see Appendix.

thousand acres for Washington, as early as July, 1773, for we find Washington's advertisement of the same, bearing the date of the 15th of July. Washington speaks of these lands as "among the first which have been surveyed." In the Maryland Gazette for March 10, 1774, may be found an official notice, dated January 27, 1774, directing gentlemen, officers, and soldiers, who claimed land under the proclamation of the 7th of October, 1763, and who had obtained warrants from the Earl of Dunmore, to appear in person or by agent, at the mouth of the Great Kanawha, on the 14th of April, and have their lands officially surveyed. The land-agents and surveyors, who went down the Kanawha upon the above errand, were stopped, or, as some say, attacked by Indians, and the hostilities which ensued brought on the bloody conflict of 1774, known as Lord Dunmore's War, which was waged by the Virginians against the Shawanese and Mingoes. This war may be regarded as the foundation of Virginia's military title to the lands back of the Alleghanies. Legal title she had not. The rumor which had been industriously circulated in January, 1774,[1] to the effect that the "new government" had fallen through, was without foundation. Lord Dunmore appears to have issued most of his patents in 1774, and to have made a violent

[1] Washington-Crawford Letters, p. 41.

effort, in the spring of that year, to assert the jurisdiction of Virginia over the entire region beyond the mountains. The attempt was made by Connolly, the agent of Lord Dunmore, to usurp authority even over territory which had formerly belonged to Pennsylvania. Connolly sought, but without success, to enforce the militia laws of Virginia in the county of Westmoreland, and to secure the country around Pittsburgh for the province of Lord Dunmore. But the conquest of the back-lands was soon effected by Virginia, and possession made her title good. Conquest and possession became accomplished facts, and against such there is no law.

By Act of Parliament, in 1774, the Crown lands north-west of the Ohio were annexed to the royal province of Quebec. It was the so-called Quebec Bill,[1] which was referred to in the Declaration of Independence as one of "their acts of pretended legislation." The King was denounced "for abolishing the free system of English laws in a neighboring province, establishing therein an arbitrary government, and enlarging its boundaries." All the American colonies felt themselves more or less aggrieved by the Quebec Bill, for lands which had been rescued from the French by the united efforts of Great Britain and America were now severed

---

[1] This document is reprinted in the Report of the Regents of the University on the Boundaries of the State of New York, pp. 90-92.

from their natural connection with the settlements of the sea-board, and formed into a vast inland province, like the ancient Louisiana of France. French law, moreover, was revived at Quebec and absolute rule seemed everywhere imminent.

But the Declaration of Independence changed the relations of things. It was the general opinion in America, that "the Crown lands" were inseparable from colonial interests, and, that in case the war should be brought to a successful issue, those States having a legal title to the western country could assert jurisdiction over the territory which fell within their respective limits. At the outbreak of the Revolution, Virginia had annexed the "County of Kentucky" to the Old Dominion, and, in 1778, after the capture of the military posts in the north-west by Colonel George Rogers Clarke,[1] in a secret expedition undertaken by Virginia at her own expense, that enterprising State proceeded to annex the lands beyond the Ohio, under the name of the County of Illinois. The military claims of Virginia were certainly very strong, but it was felt by the smaller States that an equitable consideration for the services of other colonies in defending the back country from the French, ought to induce Virginia to dispose of a

---

[1] For Clarke's own account of the Expedition, see Perkins' Annals of the West, (Cincinnati, 1846,) pp. 204-210 Clarke's commission from Patrick Henry, then Governor of Virginia, may be found in Perkins, p. 184.

portion of her western territory for the common good.

It is easy now to conceive how royal grants to Massachusetts and Connecticut of lands stretching from ocean to ocean, must have conflicted with the charter-claims and military title of Virginia to the great north-west. We have seen that Virginia's charter could be extended over the entire region beyond the Ohio. It is not necessary to quote the original charters[1] of Massachusetts and Connecticut, for, told in brief, the former's claim embraced the lands which now lie in southern Michigan and Wisconsin, or, in other words, the region comprehended by the extension westward of her present southern boundary and of her ancient northern limit,[2] which was "the latitude of a league north of the inflow of Lake Winnipiseogee in New Hampshire." The western claims of Connecticut covered portions of. Ohio, Indiana, Illinois, and Michigan.

[1] The claims of Massachusetts were based upon the charter granted by William and Mary, in 1691, and those of Connecticut upon the charter granted by Charles II. in 1662. These documents may be found in the Laws of the United States respecting the Public Lands, pp. 78, 80.

[2] This statement is from Walker's Statistical Atlas of the United States, (Areas and Political Divisions, compiled by Mr. Stocking of the Patent Office.) The text of the original charter, although somewhat obscure, seems to imply that the northern limit of Massachusetts was three miles north of the head of the *Merrimac river*. Probably Mr. Stocking has some other source of information, for his work throughout is extremely well-done, being the most reliable and concise exposition we have seen of that complicated subject, the land cessions.

The chartered rights of New York were based upon the grant of 1664 to James, Duke of York, by his brother Charles II.[1] By an agreement originally made in 1683, the boundary between Connecticut and New York was fixed at a line twenty miles distant from the Hudson river. Massachusetts agreed, in 1773, to a continuation of the same line for her western limit.[2]

The extension of charter-boundaries over the far-west by Massachusetts and Connecticut, led to no trespass on the intervening *charter*-claims of New York. Connecticut fell into a serious controversy, however, with Pennsylvania, in regard to the possession of certain lands in the northern part of the latter State, but the dispute, when brought before a court appointed by Congress, was finally decided in favor of Pennsylvania.[3] But in the western country, Massachusetts and Connecticut[4] were determined to assert their chartered rights against Virginia and the *treaty*-claims of New York, for, by virtue of various treaties with the Six Nations and allies, the latter State was asserting jurisdiction over the entire region

---

[1] See Report of the Regents of the University on the Boundaries of the State of New York, p. 11.

[2] See above Report, pp. 58, 212.

[3] January 3, 1783. See Journals of Congress, IV., p. 129, for these proceedings, which are important, as illustrating the position of the old Congress in arbitration.

[4] See Plea in Vindication of the Connecticut Title to contested lands west of New York. By Benjamin Trumbull, New Haven, 1774.

between Lake Erie and the Cumberland mountains, or, in other words, Ohio and a portion of Kentucky.[1] These claims were strengthened by the following facts: First, that the *chartered* rights of New York were merged in the Crown by the accession to the throne, in 1685, of the Duke of York as James II.; again, that the Six Nations and tributaries had put themselves under the protection of England, and that they had always been treated by the Crown as appendant to the government of New York; moreover, in the third place, the citizens of that State had borne the burden of protecting these Indians for over a hundred years.[2] New York was the great rival of Virginia in the strength and magnitude of her western claims. In fact, the chief interest of the great land-controversy turns upon the rival offers made to Congress by the two States at the instance of Maryland.

We have now in our mind's eye the conflicting claims of Virginia, Massachusetts, Connecticut, and New York to that vast region beyond the Ohio. We shall now consider, for a second topic, the process by which these various land-claims were placed upon a national basis, or, more specifically,

---

[1] See Journals of Congress, IV, p. 21. Franklin's Works, IV., 324-379.
[2] Journals of Congress, IV., p. 22.

II. THE INFLUENCE OF MARYLAND IN SECURING A GENERAL CESSION OF WESTERN TERRITORY FOR THE PUBLIC GOOD.

The immense importance of the region northwest of the Ohio as a source of national revenue, when the tide of emigration should set in, was recognized as early as 1776. Silas Deane, the agent whom the Continental Congress had sent to France, addressed a communication[1] to the Committee of Secret Correspondence, calling the attention of Congress to that triangular region described in general, by the Ohio, the Mississippi, and the parallel of Fort Detroit. "These three lines," he says, "of near one thousand miles each, include an immense territory, in a fine climate, well watered, and, by accounts, exceedingly fertile. To this I ask your attention, as a resource amply adequate, under proper regulations, for defraying the whole expense of the war."

The first move that was ever made in Congress towards the assertion of national sovereignty over this western country, was made by Maryland. On the 15th of October, 1777, exactly one month before the Articles of Confederation were proposed to the Legislatures for ratification, it was moved "that the United States in Congress assem-

[1] Diplomatic Correspondence, edited by Sparks, I., p. 79.

bled, shall have the sole and exclusive right and power to ascertain and fix the western boundary of such States as claim to the Mississippi or South Sea, and lay out the land beyond the boundary, so ascertained, into separate and independent States, from time to time, as the numbers and circumstances of the people may require."[1] *Only Maryland voted in the affirmative.* But in this motion was suggested that idea of political expansion under the sovereign control of Congress, which ultimately prevailed and constituted, upon grounds of necessity, a truly National Republic. Not only the suggestion of a firm and lasting union upon the basis of a territorial commonwealth, but the chief influence in founding such a union, must be ascribed to Maryland. And yet, strange to say, this priority of suggestion has never been noticed, and, stranger still, the constitutional importance to this country of Maryland's subsequent opposition to the land-claims has wholly escaped attention.

The original proposition that Congress should exercise sovereign power over the western country was a pioneer thought, or, as the Germans say, a *bahnbrechende Idee.* We have discovered by a careful examination of the Journals of the Old Congress, that Maryland was not only the first, but for a long time the only State, to advocate

[1] Journals of Congress, II, p. 290.

national jurisdiction over the western lands. The opposition to the establishment of a public domain, under the sovereign control of Congress was so great, at the outset, that the States possessing land claims succeeded, a few days after Maryland's motion, in adding a clause to the Ninth Article of the Confederation, to the effect that no State should be deprived of territory for the benefit of the United States.[1] In the remonstrances to this grasping policy of the larger States, by Rhode Island, New Jersey, and Delaware, we shall find that there was no thought of investing Congress with the rights of sovereignty over the Crown lands. What these States desired was either a share in the revenues arising from the western country, or, that the funds accruing from the sale of western lands should be applied towards defraying the expenses of the war. But of the western lands as the basis of republican expansion under the national jurisdiction of Congress, these States seemed to have no conception whatever. Rhode Island, in a proposed amendment to the Articles of Confederation, expressly declared that all lands within those States, the property of which before the war was vested in the Crown of Great Britain, should be disposed of for the benefit of the whole confederacy, " reserving, however, to the States

---

[1] October 27, 1777. See Journals of Congress, II., 304.

within whose limits such Crown lands may be, the entire and complete jurisdiction thereof."[1] New Jersey, in her remonstrance to the Ninth Article, while demanding that the Crown lands should be sold by Congress for defraying the expenses of the war, admits that, "The jurisdiction ought, in every instance, to belong to the respective States within the charter or determined limits of which such lands may be seated."[2] Delaware also had a keen sense of the common interest of all the States in the sale of the unoccupied western lands, but of that interest as the basis of a truly national commonwealth, she seems to have had no appreciation whatever.[3] The credit of suggesting and successfully urging in Congress, that policy which has made this country a great national commonwealth, composed of "free, convenient, and independent governments," bound together by ties of permanent territorial interests, the credit of originating this policy belongs to Maryland, and to her alone. Absolutely nothing had been effected by Rhode Island, New Jersey, and Delaware, before they ratified the Articles, towards breaking down the selfish claims of the larger States and placing the Confederation upon a national basis. Delaware, the last of all the

[1] Journals of Congress, II., p. 601.
[2] Journals of Congress, II., p. 605.
[3] Journals of Congress, III., pp. 201.

States, except Maryland, to ratify the Articles, acceded to the latter, February 22, 1779, under a mild protest, which Congress allowed to be placed on file, "provided," as was said, "it should never be considered as admitting any claim."[1] Maryland was left to fight out the battle alone, and with what success we shall shortly see.

The "Instructions" of Maryland to her delegates, which were read in Congress, May 21, 1779, after the accession of Delaware, as above stated, forbidding them to ratify the Articles of Confederation before the land-claims had been placed upon a different basis, must be regarded as one of the most important documents in our early constitutional history, for it marks the point of departure for those congressional enactments of the 6th of September and 10th of October, 1780, which were followed by such vital results for the constitutional as well as the material development of this country. From the effect of these instructions upon the acts and policy of Congress, we shall be able to trace out, from documentary evidence, that line of events which led to the great land-cessions of Virginia and New York, and to the Ordinance of 1784 for the government of the ceded territory, which Ordinance was termed "a charter of compact," the articles of which should stand as "fundamental constitutions" between the

---

[1] Journals of Congress, III., p. 209.

thirteen original States and each of the new States therein described. The following brief citations from the original document will suffice to convey its tenor and spirit, and to indicate the attitude of Maryland towards the Confederation:[1]

"Although the pressure of immediate calamities, the dread of their continuance from the appearance of disunion, and some other peculiar circumstances, may have induced some States to accede to the present confederation, contrary to their own interests and judgments, it requires no great share of foresight to predict that when those causes cease to operate, the States which have thus acceded to the confederation will consider it no longer binding, and will eagerly embrace the first occasion of asserting their just rights and securing their independence. Is it possible that those States, who are ambitiously grasping at territories, to which, in our judgment, they have not the least shadow of exclusive right, will use with greater moderation the increase of wealth and power derived from those territories, when acquired, than what they have displayed in their endeavors to acquire them? We think not. . . . . Suppose, for instance, Virginia, indisputably possessed of the extensive and fertile country to which she has set up a claim, what would be the probable consequences to Mary-

[1] Journals of Congress, III., p. 281.

land? .... Virginia, by selling on the most moderate terms, a small proportion of the lands in question, would draw into her treasury vast sums of money and .... would be enabled to lessen her taxes: lands comparatively cheap and taxes comparatively low, with the lands and taxes of an adjacent State, would quickly drain the State thus disadvantageously circumstanced, of its most useful inhabitants, its wealth; and its consequence, in the scale of the confederated States, would sink of course. A claim so injurious to more than one-half, if not the whole of the United States, ought to be supported by the clearest evidence of the right. Yet what evidences of that right have been produced? .... We are convinced, policy and justice require that a country unsettled at the commencement of this war, claimed by the British crown, and ceded to it by the treaty of Paris, if wrested from the common enemy by the blood and treasure of the thirteen States, should be considered as a common property, *subject to be parcelled out by Congress into free, convenient and independent governments*, in such manner and at such times as the wisdom of that assembly shall hereafter direct. . . . .

"We have spoken with freedom, as becomes freemen, and we sincerely wish that these our representations may make such an impression on that assembly [Congress] as to induce them to make such addition to the articles of confederation as may bring about a permanent union."[1]

In connection with the above Instructions, which were passed by the Maryland legislature as early as December 15, 1778, was sent another document, bearing the same date, which was called a Declaration. The design was, as we know from the Instructions themselves, to bring the Declaration before Congress at once, to have it printed and generally distributed among the delegates of the other States. The Instructions were to be read, in the presence of Congress, at some later period, and formally entered upon the journals of that body. We find that the Declaration was really brought forward, by the Maryland delegates, on the sixth of January, 1779, but the consideration of the same was postponed, and the document itself does not appear in the journals. In Hening's Statutes of Virginia, however, among the papers relating to the Cession of North-Western Territory, this Declaration is to be found, side by side with the Maryland Instructions, and both immediately preceding the so-called "Virginia Remonstrance," dated December 14, 1779, and an act of the New York legislature, of February 19, 1780, called "An act to facilitate the completion of the articles of confederation and

---

[1] The whole of this important and interesting document is given in the Appendix to this paper.

perpetual union, among the United States of America."[1] As the latter documents reveal the first practical results of Maryland's policy in opposing the land-claims, it is necessary to investigate their origin.

In May, 1779, the same month, it will be remembered, that the Maryland Instructions were read before Congress, the Virginia legislature passed an act for establishing a Land Office and for ascertaining the terms upon which land-grants should be issued.[2] It was declared that vacant western territory, belonging to Virginia, should be sold at the rate of forty pounds for every hundred acres. In another act, passed about the same time, the patents issued to officers and soldiers, under the proclamation of 1763, by any royal governor of Virginia, were declared valid, but all unpatented surveys were to be held null and void; except in the case of settlers actually occupying lands to which no person had a legal title. Such settlers were to be allowed four hundred acres, on the condition of entering their claims at the Land Office. By such measures was Virginia proceeding to dispose of the western lands, to which Maryland had set up a claim in the interest of the United States. But Virginia was trespassing on the legal rights of the great

---

[1] Hening, Virginia Statutes at Large, X , pp. 549-61.
[2] Hening, Virginia Statutes at Large, X., pp. 50-65.

land-companies, particularly upon the claims of the Vandalia to Walpole's Grant, which we have previously described. On the fourteenth of September, 1779, a memorial was read to Congress, in behalf of the interests of Thomas Walpole and his associates. This memorial was referred to a committee on the eighth of October, and the favorable report which was subsequently made upon the claims of American members of the Vandalia Company has already been mentioned.[1] But, on the thirtieth of October, long before this committee had reported, the following resolution was introduced by *Mr. William Paca, of Maryland, and seconded by his colleague, Mr. George Plater:*

"WHEREAS, the appropriation of vacant lands by the several states during the continuance of the war will, in the opinion of Congress, be attended with great mischiefs; therefore,

Resolved, That it be earnestly recommended to the State of Virginia, to re-consider their late act of assembly for opening their land-office; and that it be recommended to the said state, and all other states similarly circumstanced, to forbear settling or issuing warrants for unappropriated lands, or granting the same during the continuance of the present war."[2]

---

[1] See p. 17.
[2] Journals of Congress, III, p. 384.

This resolution was adopted, only Virginia and North Carolina voting in the negative. The New York delegates were divided.

These steps bring us to the famous Remonstrance, which was addressed "by the General Assembly of Virginia to the delegates of the United American States in Congress assembled." The connecting link between the Maryland Instructions and Virginia's Remonstrance, is supplied by the above Resolution of Mr. Paca. Virginia protests against the idea of Congress exercising *jurisdiction*, or any right of adjudication concerning the petitions of the Vandalia or Indiana landcompanies, or upon "*any other matter*," subversive of the internal policy of Virginia or any of the United States. But in this Remonstrance, Virginia declares herself "ready to listen to any just and reasonable propositions for removing the *ostensible* causes of delay to the complete ratification of the confederation."[1] The word *ostensible* is italicized in the original document and refers, of course, to Maryland, for this State was now the only one which had not ratified the Articles. Manifestly, the influence of Maryland was, at last, beginning to tell. It was the sturdy opposition of this State to the grasping[2] claims of Virginia and

[1] Hening, Virginia Statutes at Large, X., pp. 357-59.
[2] Virginians who object to this phrase are referred to the Writings of Washington, IX., p. 33, where, in a letter to Jefferson, he says: "I am not less in sentiment with you respecting the impolicy of this State's *grasping* at more territory than they are competent to the government of."

the larger States, which first awakened a readiness for compromise in the matter of land-claims. Hening says Maryland "*insisted* that the States, claiming these western territories, should bring them into the common stock, for the benefit of the whole Union."[1] Howison, the most recent historian of Virginia, declares, that "Maryland was inflexible and refused to become a party [to the Confederation] until the claims of the States should be on a satisfactory basis."[2]

The readiness of Virginia to do something to remove the "*ostensible cause*" of delay on Maryland's part, indicates that her land-claims were becoming less positive. But the act of the legislature of New York "to facilitate the completion of the Articles of Confederation," shows most decidedly that Maryland's cause was prevailing. The historic connection of this measure with the influence of Maryland delegates in Congress has never been shown, but from materials now accessible in a letter of General Schuyler, first published in 1873, in the Report of the Regents of the University on the Boundaries of the State of New York, we think this connection may fairly be demonstrated. General Schuyler was delegate to Congress from New York in 1779. On the twenty-ninth of January, 1780, he addressed a

---

[1] Hening, Virginia Statutes at Large, X., p. 548.
[2] Howison, History of Virginia, II., p. 286.

letter from Albany, to the New York legislature, which gives us the key to their act of the nineteenth of February. General Schuyler had been advocating in Congress a treaty with the Cayuga Indians. "Whilst the report of the committee on the business I have alluded to," he says, "was under consideration, *a member* moved, in substance, that the Commissioners for Indian Affairs in the Northern Department should require from the Indians of the Six Nations, as a preliminary Article, a cession of part of their country, and that the territory so to be ceded should be for the benefit of the United States in general and grantable by Congress." The first question is, who was this member? The policy recommended in the above motion is very suggestive of some Maryland delegate. On referring to the Journals of Congress for the above discussion, we find two motions on the subject mentioned by General Schuyler; the first was made by *Mr. Forbes of Maryland* and seconded by Mr. Houston of New Jersey; the other was made by Mr. Marchant of Rhode Island and seconded by *Mr. Forbes*. Both motions were defeated, but that which alarmed General Schuyler and of which he thought it necessary to unburden himself to his constituents, was simply this: "we had a few days after," he says, "a convincing proof that an idea prevailed that this and some other States ought to be divested of part of their territory for the benefit of the United States, when *a member* afforded us the perusal of a resolution, for which he intended, to move the House, purporting that all the lands within the limits of any of the United States, heretofore grantable by the king of Great Britain whilst these States (then Colonies) were in the dominion of that prince, and which had not been granted to individuals, should be considered as the *joint property* of the United States and disposed of by Congress for the benefit of the whole Confederacy." We have searched in vain for the above resolution in the Journals of Congress, although, from internal evidence, there is little doubt but that it came from the same source as the original motion, which so alarmed General Schuyler.

The chief importance which this letter to the New York legislature has for us, in this connection, is the revelation it affords of the growing influence of the Maryland policy in Congress. General Schuyler confesses that the opposition to the original motion [of Mr. Forbes] was chiefly based upon the inexpediency of such an assertion of Congressional authority while endeavoring to secure a reconciliation with the Indians. In private conversation, the General had ascertained that certain gentlemen, who represented States in the same circumstances as New York in the matter of land-claims, were inclined to support the resolution in its new form. It was urged by the friends of the proposed resolution, that a reasonable limitation of the land-claims would prevent controversy "*and remove the obstacle which prevented the completion of the Confederation.*" General Schuyler says he endeavored, with great discretion, to ascertain the idea of the advocates of this measure as to what would constitute a reasonable limitation of the claims. "This they gave," he says, "by exhibiting a map of the country, on which they drew a line from the north-west corner of Pennsylvania (which in that map was laid down as on Lake Erie) through the strait that leads to Ontario and through that Lake and down the St. Lawrence to the forty-fifth degree of latitude, for the bounds of the State in that quarter. Virginia, the two Carolinas, and Georgia, they proposed to restrict by the Alleghany Mountains, or at farthest by the Ohio, to where that river enters the Mississippi and by the latter river to the south bounds of Georgia—That all the Territory to the west of these limits should become the *property* of the Confederacy. We found this matter had been in contemplation some time, the delegates from North Carolina having then already requested instructions from their constituents on the subject, and my colleagues were in sentiment with me that it should be humbly submitted to the Legislature, if it would not be proper to communicate their pleasure in the premises by way of instruction to their servants in Congress." Such were the appeals of congressmen to their constituents before national interests were fully recognized and before National Government was developed from grounds of necessity. But this letter clearly indicates the influence of the Maryland idea and the growth of a truly national sentiment in Congress, which was destined to find expression in that famous resolution of the sixth of September, 1780, wherein a general land-cession was first recommended to the States holding title to western territory.

It will be seen upon examination of the proceedings of the New York legislature,[1] that this letter from General Schuyler was the immediate occasion of the passage of an act by the Senate and Assembly of that State, called "An act to facilitate the completion of the articles of confederation and perpetual union among the United States of America." In this act, which was passed the nineteenth of February, 1780, New York authorized her delegates in Congress to make either an unreserved or a limited cession of her western lands according as these delegates should deem it

---

[1] Reprinted in full in the Report of the Regents of the University on the Boundaries of the State of New York, pp. 141-149. For the act itself see Journals of Congress, III., p. 582.

expedient. This act was read in Congress on the seventh of March.

On the sixth of September, 1780, a memorable date in the history of the land-question, a report was made on the Maryland Instructions, the Virginia Remonstrance, and the above Act of the New York legislature. Although this report did not recommend an examination of the points at issue between Maryland and Virginia, it did recommend a liberal cession of western lands by all states which laid claim to such possessions. "It appears more advisable," said the committee, "to press upon those states which can remove the embarrassments respecting the western country, a liberal surrender of a portion of their territorial claims, since they cannot be preserved entire without endangering the *stability* of the general confederacy; to remind them how indispensably necessary it is *to establish the federal union on a fixed and permanent basis, and on principles acceptable to all its respective members;* how essential to public credit and confidence, to the support of our army, to our tranquility at home, our reputation abroad, to our very existence as a free, sovereign and independent people; that they are fully persuaded the wisdom of the respective legislatures will lead them to a full and impartial consideration of a subject so interesting to the United States, and *so necessary to the happy establishment of the federal union;* that they are confirmed in these expectations by a review of the before-mentioned act of the legislature of New York, submitted to their consideration; that this act is expressly calculated to accelerate the Federal alliance, by removing, as far as depends on that state, the impediment arising from the western country, and for that purpose to yield up a portion of territorial claim for the general benefit; Whereupon

Resolved, That copies of the several papers referred to the committee be transmitted, with a copy of the report, to the legislatures of the several states, and that it be earnestly recommended to those states, who have claims to the western country, to pass such laws, and give their delegates in Congress such powers as may effectually remove the *only obstacle* to a final ratification of the articles of confederation; and *that the legislature of Maryland be earnestly requested to authorize their delegates in Congress to subscribe the said articles.*"[1]

But Maryland awaited some definite proposals from Virginia and the other states which laid claim to the western lands. Madison, in a letter of September 12, 1780, remarks with great significance, "As these exclusive claims formed the only obstacle with Maryland, there is no doubt that a compliance with this recommendation [of

[1] Journals of Congress, III., p. 516.

Congress] will bring her into the Confederation."[1] Connecticut[2] soon offered a cession of western lands, provided that she might retain the jurisdiction. It is a remarkable fact that, at this period, Alexander Hamilton should have favored such a reservation by states ceding lands to the Confederation. In his proposals for constitutional reform, in a letter to James Duane, of New York, dated September 3, 1780, he says that Congress should be invested with the whole or a portion of the western lands as a basis of future revenue, "*reserving the jurisdiction to the States by whom they are granted.*[3]"

But the original idea of Maryland that the western country should " be parcelled out by Congress into free, convenient, and independent governments," was destined to prevail. On the tenth

[1] Madison Papers, p. 50.
[2] This offer was made October 10, 1780. The terms of the legislative act show conclusively that the Maryland Instructions were exercising their influence upon the country. "This Assembly taking into their consideration a Resolution of Congress of the 6th of September last, recommending to the several States which have vacant unappropriated Lands, lying within the Limits of their respective Charters and Claims, to adopt measures which may *effectually remove the obstacle that prevents the ratification of the Articles of confederation*, together with the Papers from the States of New York, Maryland and Virginia, which accompanied the same, and being anxious for the accomplishment of an event most desirable and important to the Liberty and Independence of this rising Empire, will do everything in their power to facilitate the same notwithstanding the objections which they have to several parts of it. *Resolved, etc.*
MS. Laws of Conn. First printed in Report of the Regents of the University on the Boundaries of the State of New York, p. 157 (1873.)
[3] Works of Hamilton, I., p. 157.

of October, it was resolved by Congress that those lands which should be ceded in accordance with the recommendation of the sixth of September, should not only be disposed of for the benefit of the Confederation, but should be formed into distinct republican states, which should become members of the federal union and have the same rights of sovereignty as the other states.[1] It was added, probably as an inducement to Virginia to cede her western lands, that Congress would reimburse any particular state for expenses incurred, since the commencement of the war, in subduing or defending any part of the western territory. The expedition of George Rogers Clarke, for the reduction of the north-western posts, had been undertaken by Virginia without aid from Congress or from the Continental army, and this fact had been urged by Virginia as a crowning title to the lands north-west of the Ohio. But Virginia seems to have acted upon the above recommendation of Congress, for by her act[2] of the second of January, 1781, she offered to cede to the Confederation complete jurisdiction over all lands north-west of the Ohio on certain conditions, the first of which, in regard to the disposition of territory and the formation of distinct republican

---

[1] Journals of Congress, III., p. 535.
[2] Hening, Virginia Statutes at Large, X., p. 564, or Journals of Congress, IV., p. 265.

states, was taken almost verbatim from the above resolutions of Congress.

Howison, the historian of Virginia, admits that "this cession was made with the immediate design of inducing all the states to become parties to the Confederation" and "the effect of Virginia's offer," he asserts, "was in accordance with the hopes of its advocates, for Maryland became a party to the Confederation."[1] If a desire to facilitate the completion of the union was indeed the motive of the proposed land cessions by New York and Virginia, as the language of their legislative acts certainly justifies us in supposing, then alone the attitude of Maryland towards the Confederation must be regarded as a sufficient occasion for their action, for Maryland was the only state which had not ratified the Articles. The keystone to the old Confederation was not laid until Maryland had virtually effected her object and secured the offer of land cessions to the United States from Virginia, as well as from New York and Connecticut. As Hildreth says of Maryland, "she made a determined stand, steadily refusing her assent to the Confederation, without some guarantee that the equitable right of the union to these western regions should be respected."[2]

---

[1] Howison, History of Virginia, II., p. 282.
[2] Hildreth, History of the United States, III., p. 399.

We may doubt, however whether the action of Virginia, independent of the previous offer by New York, would have been sufficient to persuade Maryland to join the Confederation, for Virginia had attached such obnoxious conditions[1] to her proposed cession, that Congress as well as Maryland were dissatisfied with the same. Virginia demanded, among other things, that Congress should guarantee to her the undisturbed possession of all lands south-east of the Ohio and that claims of other parties to the north-west territory should be annulled as infringing upon the chartered rights of Virginia, for, in making the proposed cession, Virginia evidently desired to put the Confederation under as heavy an obligation as possible. These conditions which Congress pronounced "incompatible with the honor, interests and peace of the United States,"[2] led to an encouragement of the New York offer, which was formally made in Congress, March 1, 1781. On that very day, Maryland ratified the Articles and the first legal union of the United States was complete. The coincidence in dates is too striking to admit of any other explanation than that Maryland and New York were acting with a mutual understanding. An act authorizing the delegates from Maryland to subscribe to the

---

[1] Journals of Congress, IV, p. 266.
[2] Journals of Congress, IV., p. 22.

Articles had been read in Congress on the twelfth of February. This act had been passed by the legislature of that state ten days[1] before indicating that the Virginia offer, of January 2, had not been wholly without influence upon Maryland, although her delegates appear to have delayed signing the Articles until the New York offer had been fully secured and the land question had been placed upon a national basis. That Maryland was dissatisfied with the partial and illiberal cession by Virginia is evident from the closing paragraph of the above mentioned act of her legislature. " It is hereby declared, that, by acceding to the said Confederation, this State doth not relinquish, or intend to relinquish any right or interest she hath, with the other united or confederated states, to the back country; but claims the same as fully as was done by the legislature of this state, in their declaration which stands entered on the Journals of Congress." Maryland furthermore declared that no Article of the Confederation could or ought to bind her or any other state to guarantee *jurisdiction* over the back lands to any individual member of the confederacy.[2]

The offer of Virginia, reserving to herself jurisdiction over the County of Kentucky; the offer

---

[1] February 2, 1781. Journals of Congress, III., pp. 576–7.
[2] The Act of the Maryland Legislature authorizing their delegates to subscribe to the Articles of Confederation is re-printed in our Appendix.

of Connecticut, withholding jurisdiction over all her back lands; and the offer of New York, untrammeled by burdensome conditions and conferring upon Congress complete jurisdiction over her entire western territory, these three offers were now prominently before the country. The completion of the union by Maryland had occasioned great rejoicing throughout the states and public sentiment was fast ripening for a truly national policy with reference to the disposal of the western lands. If we examine the Madison Papers and the Journals of Congress from this time onward to 1783 we shall find that congressional politics seem to turn upon three questions, (1,) finance, (2,) the disposal of the western lands, and (3,) the admission of Vermont into the union. We shall find that the question of providing for the public debt was inseparably connected with the sale of the western lands, and that the real reason why Vermont was excluded from the union until 1791, is to be sought for in the influence which the New York land cession exerted upon party feeling in Congress. These matters cannot be traced out here and we must briefly pass over the acceptance of the New York and Virginia cessions, which occasioned so much debate and controversy between the years 1781 and 1783.

A committee that had been appointed by Congress to inquire into the claims of the different states and land companies, reported May 1, 1782, in favor of accepting the offer of New York, which had been made ten months before, on the very day Maryland had formally acceded to the Confederation. One of the chief reasons assigned by the above committee, why the offer of New York should be preferred to that of Virginia, was that Congress, by accepting the New York cession, would acquire *jurisdiction*[1] over the whole western territory belonging to the Six Nations and their allies, whose lands, as we have seen, extended from Lake Erie to the Cumberland Mountains, thus covering the lands south-east of the Ohio, which Virginia desired to retain within her own jurisdiction. On the twenty-ninth of October, 1782, *Mr. Daniel Carroll, of Maryland*, moved that Congress accept the right, title, jurisdiction, and claim of New York, as ceded by the agents of that state on the first of March, 1781. By the adoption of this motion, it was supposed that the offers of Connecticut and Virginia had received a decided rebuff, but, in the end, it was found necessary to conciliate Virginia, before proceeding to dispose of the western lands. On the thirteenth day of September, 1783, it was voted by Congress to accept the cession offered by Virginia, of the territory north-west of the Ohio, provided that state would waive the obnoxious conditions con-

[1] Journals of Congress, IV, p. 22.

cerning the *guaranty* of Virginia's boundary, and the annulling of all other titles to the north-west territory. Virginia modified her conditions as requested, and on the twentieth of October, 1783,[1] empowered her delegates in Congress to make the cession, which was done by Thomas Jefferson, and others, March 1, 1784, just three years after the accession of Maryland to the Confederation.

Massachusetts ceded her western lands, together with jurisdiction over the same, April 19, 1785, and Connecticut followed Sept. 14, 1786, reserving, however, certain lands south of Lake Erie for educational and other purposes. This was the so-called "Connecticut Reserve," a tract nearly as large as the present State of Connecticut. Washington strongly condemned this compromise[2] and Mr. Grayson said it was a clear loss to the United States of about six million acres already ceded by Virginia and New York. Connecticut granted five hundred thousand acres of this Reserve to certain of her citizens, whose property had been burned or destroyed during the Revolution and the lands thus granted were known as the Fire Lands. The remainder of the Reserve was sold in 1795 for $1,200,000, which sum has been used for schools and colleges. Jurisdiction over this tract was finally ceded to Congress, May 30, 1800,

---
[1] See Hening's Statutes, XI., pp. 326-28.
[2] Writings of Washington, IX., p. 178.

and thus, at the close of the century, the accession of north-west territory was complete.[1]

We have thus traced the process by which the great land cessions were effected and have seen that it was primarily the opposition of Maryland to the grasping claims of Virginia, which put the train of compromise and land cessions in motion. We have seen that New York first offered to cede her western territory in order "to facilitate the completion of the Articles of Confederation," and, that on the very day her offer was formally made in Congress, *Maryland laid the key-stone of the Confederation* and, as we shall attempt to show, of the American Union. We come now to the third and last topic of our research, viz:

---

[1] For deed of cession, see Land Laws of the United States, p. 107. Hon. James A. Garfield's paper on the "Discovery and Ownership of the North-western Territory, and Settlement of the Western Reserve," contains some valuable matter. It is No. 20 of the publications of the Western Reserve and Northern Ohio Historical Society, 1874.

Although, in this paper, we are chiefly concerned with the Accession of the North-west Territory, we have thought it not improper to append the dates of those land cessions which were immediately occasioned by the above, and of those later accessions, by purchase or conquest, which have more than doubled our National Domain:

South Carolina Cession,	1787
North Carolina "	1790
Georgia "	1802
Louisiana Purchase,	1803
Spanish Cession of Florida,	1819
Texas Annexation,	1845
First Mexican Cession,	1848
Texas Cession,	1850
Second Mexican Cession, or the Gadsden Purchase,	1853
Alaska,	1867

III. The Origin of our Territorial Government and the true Basis of National Sovereignty.

We have seen that Maryland first suggested the idea of investing Congress with complete sovereignty over the western country, and that it was primarily through her influence that the land cessions were effected. The constitutional importance of this acquisition of territory by the Confederation has never been brought out in its true light and proper historic connections. Writers have told us, indeed, how a meeting of commissioners from Maryland and Virginia at Alexandria, in 1785, to discuss and concert uniform commercial regulations for these two states, was the original point of departure which led to the Annapolis and Philadelphia Conventions, and hence to the adoption of the present constitution, but no investigator appears to have discovered the intimate connection between the Virginia land cession of 1784, which we have just noticed, and this friendly conference between Maryland and Virginia, from which such great events are said to flow. What light, for example, is thrown upon that meeting in Alexandria by the following passage from a letter of James Madison to Thomas Jefferson, written in March, 1784, about a fortnight after the Virginia cession, but a full year before the above commercial convention was brought about! "The good humor," Madison[1] says, "into which the cession of the back lands must have put Maryland, forms an apt crisis for any negotiations which may be necessary." We have heard also, that these Alexandria commissioners went to Mount Vernon and there conferred with George Washington, who, as there is some reason to believe, first suggested a national convention to concert uniform commercial regulations for the whole country; but no one has ever shown how the first steps towards the organization of our public domain into new states were also suggested by George Washington and not by Thomas Jefferson, as is commonly supposed. The idea of parcelling out the western country "into free, convenient and independent governments" was first proclaimed by Maryland in those famous Instructions to her delegates, but the first definite *plan* for the formation of new states in the west is to be found in a letter[2] written the seventh of September, 1783, by General Washington to James Duane, member of Congress from New York. The letter contains a series of wise observations concerning "the line of conduct proper to be observed, not only towards

[1] Writings of Madison, I., p. 74.
[2] Sparks' Life and Writings of Washington, VIII., p. 477.

the Indians, but for the government of the citizens of America in their settlement of the western country." Washington's suggestions in regard to laying out two new states are particularly interesting and valuable from an historical point of view, because the conformation which he recommends for them bears a striking resemblance to the present shape of Ohio and Michigan, whereas Jefferson's original suggestions for ten states in the north-west, lying in tiers, between meridians and parallels of latitude, was never adopted, and fortunately, perhaps, for the reputation of the country; for Jefferson would have named these states: Sylvania, Michigania, Chersonesus, Assenisipia, Metropotamia, Illinoia, Saratoga, Washington, Polypotamia, and Pelisipia![1] The practical suggestions of George Washington with reference to adopting an Indian policy and some definite scheme for organizing the western territory, were adopted almost word for word in a series of resolutions by Congress, which are to be found in the Secret Journals of that body, under the date of October 15, 1783.[2] In referring to the regular Journal of Congress for the above date, we find the report of a committee consisting of Mr. Duane,

[1] National Intelligencer, August 26, 1847. Notes on the Ordinance of 1787, by Peter Force. Sparks' Life and Writings of Washington, IX., p. 48.

[2] Dr. Austin Scott, of the Johns Hopkins University, was the first to discover this remarkable coincidence.

of New York, Mr. Peters, of Pennsylvania, *Mr. Daniel*[1] *Carroll, of Maryland*, and two other gentlemen, to which committee sundry letters and papers concerning Indian affairs had been referred. The committee *acknowledge in their report that they have conferred with the commander-in-chief*. When now we recall the fact that the chairman of the above committee was James Duane, the very man to whom Washington addressed his letter of the seventh of September, the whole matter clears up and George Washington stands revealed as the moving spirit in the first active measures for the organization of the Public Lands.

Six days after the date of Washington's letter to James Duane, the report of the committee on the Virginia cession was called up and it was voted by Congress to accept Virginia's offer under the conditions which we have previously stated. That which interests us in this connection is the attempt made by *Mr. Carroll, of Maryland*, to postpone the consideration of the Virginia offer for the adoption of an important resolution in which the rights of absolute sovereignty over the western territory are claimed

---

[1] Charles Carroll of Carrollton left Congress in 1778. Daniel Carroll was delegate from 1780 to 1784 and again from 1789 to 1791. He signed the Articles of Confederation in the name of Maryland, and also the present Constitution. He seems to have exercised considerable influence in Congress. He was three times elected chairman and once appointed commissioner to treat with the Southern Indians, but declined the office on account of ill-health.

for the United States, "as one undivided and independent nation, with all and every power and right exercised by the king of Great Britain over the said territory." Mr. Carroll proposed in his resolution the appointment of a committee to report on the most eligible parcels of land for the formation of one or more convenient and independent states. Although unsuccessful, this is the boldest attempt that is recorded on the Journals of Congress for the *assertion of national sovereignty and of the rights of eminent domain over the western territory*.[1]

About one month later, Congress having voted to accept the Virginia offer, on certain conditions, we find the above committee on Indian affairs, of which Mr. Duane, of New York, was chairman and *Mr. Carroll of Maryland* a member, reporting a series of resolutions in which the influence of Washington may be clearly traced. It was declared to be a wise and necessary measure to erect a district of the western territory into a distinct government, and it was resolved that a committee should be appointed to report a plan for connecting with the Confederation by a temporary government, the inhabitants of the new district until their number and circumstances should entitle them to form a permanent constitution for themselves, on republican principles

---

[1] Journals of Congress, IV., pp. 263-265.

and, as citizens of a free, sovereign, and independent state, to be admitted into the union. In these resolutions lies the germ of Jefferson's ordinance, which was reported March 1, 1784. This fact and the connection of Duane's resolutions with the original suggestions by George Washington have never before been brought out. The influence exerted by the sage of Mount Vernon upon the Alexandria commissioners towards the practical reform of our commercial regulations was like that exercised in the above scheme for establishing a territorial government north-west of the Ohio, even before that territory had been fully ceded. Washington's plans were what the Germans would call "*bahnbrechend.*" His suggestions were the pioneer-thoughts of genius; they opened up the ways and pointed out the means.

We shall not be able in this paper to take up the Ordinance of 1784, much less that of 1787, for the government of the North West Territory. Both of these themes are extremely important and require a careful investigation. We must be content with having found the missing link which connects the Ordinance of 1784 with the practical suggestions of George Washington and with the original idea of Maryland that Congress should assume National Sovereignty over the western territory. Although this idea, which Maryland proclaimed as early as 1777, did not obtain that formal recognition which Mr. Carroll hoped to secure by his resolution of the thirteenth of September, 1783, yet, in the nature of things, arose a sovereign relation between the people of the United States and this territorial commonwealth in the west.

And just here lies the immense significance of this acquisition of Public Lands. It led to the exercise of National Sovereignty in the sense of eminent domain, a power totally foreign to the Articles of Confederation. Congress had not the slightest authority to organize a government for the western territory. The Ordinance of 1784 was never referred to the States for ratification, and yet its articles were termed a "charter of compact" and it was declared that they should stand as "*fundamental constitutions*"[1] between the thirteen original states and each of the new states therein described. Consider, moreover, the importance of the Ordinance of 1787 in establishing the bulwarks of free soil beyond the Ohio and in providing for the educational interests of the Great North-West. "I doubt," says Daniel Webster,[2] "whether one single law of any lawgiver, ancient or modern, has produced effects of

---

[1] Journals of Congress, IV., p. 380.
[2] Webster's Works, III., p. 263. Webster was mistaken in ascribing the authorship of this famous Ordinance to Nathan Dane. Mr. W. F. Poole, of Chicago, in his admirable monograph on the Ordinance of 1787

more distinct, marked, and lasting character than the Ordinance of 1787."

This Ordinance is an exhibition of national sovereignty on the grandest scale, yet where was the authority for it? The present Constitution had not been adopted and yet Congress was proceeding to legislate on national interests with a boldness which might well have startled those who believed in the doctrine that Government derives its just powers from the consent of the governed. Madison, in a contribution to the Federalist, avails himself of this fact, that Congress was already exercising sovereignty as an argument for establishing constitutional government with defined powers. "It is now no longer a point of speculation and hope," he says, "that the western territory is a mine of vast wealth to the United States: .... Congress have assumed the administration of this stock. They have begun to render it productive. Congress have undertaken to do more:—they have proceeded to form

(see North American Review, April, 1876) has proved conclusively that Mr. Dane could not have been the author, and has made out a strong case for Dr. Manasseh Cutler, of Massachusetts. The same view is taken in a paper read before the New Jersey Historical Society, May 16, 1872. See Proceedings of that society, Second Series (1867–74) III., p. 76. There is a paper on the "Ordinance of 1787" by Edward Coles, formerly governor of Illinois (1822-26,) which was read before the Pennsylvania Historical Society, June 9, 1856 and was issued by the Press of the Society in that year. It contains, however, many errors, which Mr. Poole has now set aside. Poole's article is reprinted in pamphlet form by Welch, Bigelow & Co., Cambridge, 1876.

new states; to erect temporary governments; to
appoint officers for them; and to prescribe the
conditions on which such states shall be admitted
into the confederacy. All this has been done: and
done *without the least color of constitutional authority.*
Yet no blame has been whispered: no alarm has
been sounded. A great and independent fund of
revenue is passing into the hands of a single body
of men, who can raise troops to an indefinite
number, and appropriate money to their support
for an indefinite period of time . . . . . I mean
not by anything here said to throw censure on the
measures which have been pursued by Congress.
I am sensible they could not have done otherwise.
The public interest, the necessity of the case,
imposed upon them the task of overleaping their
constitutional limits."[1]

Madison here reveals the true basis of political
sovereignty. Public good and the necessities of
the territorial situation are the sovereign law of
every political commonwealth. The fundamental
idea of a republic is the common good (respublica)
and the radical notion of politics ($πόλις$) is government
of *civil* society, which is first united by
material interests. The good old word *commonwealth*
best expresses to the English mind not only

[1] Federalist No. XXXVIII., Jan. 15, 1788. (Edition of J. C. Hamilton, 1875, p. 299.)

the controlling principle of state-life which is the common weal, but the necessary condition of political existence which is the possession of a common country or territorial domain. It was the public interest of the original states in the western lands, as a means of satisfying army claims and defraying the expenses of the war, which held together thirteen *de facto* sovereign powers after independence had been achieved and the recommendations of Congress had become a laughing-stock. The Confederation, in itself, was a mere league and Congress little more than a committee of public safety appointed by thirteen colonies which desired territorial independence in common but self-government and state-sovereignty for each. When the war was over, these jealous powers would have fallen apart if there had been no other influence than Congress to hold them together. It was only external pressure which had united the colonies, and without *permament territorial interests* Congress would have been, indeed, "a shadow without the substance," as Washington termed it, and the country, "one nation to-day and thirteen to-morrow," as best suited the purposes of individual states. But out of this sovereign relation which was established between the United States and their public domain, was developed a truly national sovereignty. Madison[1] speaks of this new manifestation of energy as "an excrescent power," growing "out of the lifeless mass" of the Confederation, and yet he justifies the acts of Congress for the government of the western territory, on grounds of necessity and of the public good. A surer foundation for national sovereignty has never been discovered. Political science no longer defends the Social Contract as the basis of government. The best writers of our day reject those atomistic theories of State, which would derive national sovereignty from compact, or arithmetical majorities, and not from the commonwealth, or the solidarity of public interests.

Government is derived from the living necessities and united interests of a people. The State does not rest upon compact or written constitutions. There is something more fundamental than delegated powers or chartered sovereignty. The state is grounded upon that community of material interests which arises from the *permanent* relation of a people to some fixed territory. Government can exist among men who have no enduring interest in land, as, for example, among nomadic hordes, but the State stands firm, although capable of organic development. Dynasties may change and the principles of Government become wholly

[1] Federalist, No. XXXVIII., p. 299.

republican, but En*gland* would endure so long as a sovereign and abiding relation subsists between the English people and their island domain.[1] The element of continuity in every state-life is directly dependent upon this sovereign relation between a people and some fixed territory. Remove a people from their domain and you destroy their state. If the Puritans of Massachusetts had accepted the invitation[2] of Lord Baltimore and removed to Maryland, it is to be presumed that Plymouth Rock and the Bay State would have fallen into oblivion or acquired a totally different place in New England history. The Pilgrims' Compact is often cited as an example of the "Social Contract," but suppose the people of New England had accepted Cromwell's advice[3] and migrated to tropical Jamaica, is it likely that their compact would have established a *New England* in that fertile island, which pours its wealth so "prodigally into the lap of industry?" Territorial influences enter so largely into the constitution and political life of a state that we cannot conceive of a political commonwealth as existing independently of certain

[1] Das Staatsgebiet ist entschieden für den Staat und seine Entwickelung von fundamentaler Bedeutung, was schon daraus hervorgeht, dass man gewöhnlich in der Benennung den Staat mit demselben identificirt. Winkler, Das Staatsgebiet. Eine cultur-geographische Studie, p. 3, Leipzig, 1877.
[2] Bancroft, History of the United States, I., p. 253.
[3] Bancroft, History of the United States, I., p. 446.

material conditions.[1] It is, therefore, but a partial truth when the lawyer-poet[2] says:

> Men who their duties know,
> But know their rights and knowing dare maintain,
> * * * * * * *
> These constitute a state.

Although a free and sovereign people is undoubtedly the animating life of the American Republic, yet that life has a *material basis* of which writers on American constitutional history have taken too little cognizance. No state without a people, but no state without land:[3] these are the fundamental principles of political science and were recognized as early as the days of Aristotle.[4] The common interest of all the states in our western territory was the first truly national commonwealth upon American shores, for it bound these states together into a *permanent* political union and established a sovereign relation between the United States and a territorial domain. Without public interests of a solid and lasting character the military union of thirteen *de facto* sovereign powers would never have grown into a

---

[1] Der Staat .... geht aus natürlichen Bedingungen hervor; physische Verhältnisse sind die Grundlage seiner Existenz und Entwickelung. Winkler, Das Staatsgebiet, p. 3.

[2] Sir William Jones, first translator of the Laws of Manu, and a pioneer of Comparative Jurisprudence as well as of Comparative Philology.

[3] Bluntschli, *Statslehre für Gebildete*, p. 12 " Kein Stat ohne Land." See also *Lehre vom Modernen Stat.* I., p. 15. (Stuttgart, 1875.)

[4] Aristotle, Polit. III., 5, 14.

national union with inherent rights of sovereignty. "Constitutions are not made," says Sir James Macintosh, "they grow." The American Republic is the product, not of concessions or concensus, but of *development from the existing relations of things*. Political interests of a lasting character were entailed upon the Confederation by the possession of a territorial commonwealth. "From the very origin of the government," said Daniel Webster in his first great speech on the Public Lands in answer to Mr. Hayne of South Carolina, "From the very origin of the government these western lands and the just protection of those who had settled or should settle on them, have been the leading objects in our policy."[1]

But we have seen that even before the adoption of our present form of government, these western lands constituted the most vital and absorbing question in American politics. The acquisition of a territorial commonwealth by these states was the *foundation of a permanent union;* it was the first solid arch upon which the framers of our Constitution could build.

When now we consider the practical results arising from Maryland's prudence in laying the key-stone to the old Confederation only after the land-claims of the larger states had, through her influence, been placed upon a national basis, we

[1] Webster's Works, III., p. 251.

may say, with truth, that it was a National Commonwealth which Maryland founded. It seems strange that so little attention has been devoted to the question of Public Lands[1] and their influence upon the constitutional development of this country. In view of the fact that the greatest conflict in American politics has been for the organization of the west upon the principles of the Ordinance of 1787, it would seem as though the subject of the Territorial Commonwealth of the American Union might justly demand from our students of history something more than "the cold respect of a passing glance."

---

[1] The author is indebted to Dr. Emil Otto, of Heidelberg, for a copy of a dissertation on *Die Public Lands der Vereinigten Staaten von Nord-Amerika. Inaugural-Dissertation zur Erlangung der Doctorwürde von der juristischen Facultät der Friedrich - Wilhelms - Universität zu Berlin,* . . . . . *von James P. Foster aus New-York.* Berlin, 19 April, 1877. Although Dr. Foster has anticipated his countryman and former fellow-student, by scientifically investigating the question of "Public Lands," still, as a lawyer, he has considered *legal relations* rather than *historic processes*, and has not touched at all upon the points made in this article.

The Ordinance of 1787 is but the legal outcome of Maryland's successful policy in advocating National Sovereignty over the Western Lands. The leading principles of this Ordinance are now recognized in all parts of our country, but those principles were long ago approved of by Maryland, although in a somewhat singular manner. In 1833, when the vessel sailed which carried to western Africa the emigrants who were to establish, under the auspices of the Maryland State Colonization Society, the colony of Maryland in Liberia, at Cape Palmas, the agent of the society took with him two documents, the one a Constitution, containing a Bill of Rights, and the other an Ordinance for the government of the territory about to be acquired. The work of preparing these instruments was done by Mr. John H. B. Latrobe, then the corresponding secretary of the society and one of its most active members. The animating principles of these instruments, and, to some extent, their very form and substance, were furnished by the famous Ordinance of 1787. When the Constitution and Ordinance were reported to the society by the secretary, they were unanimously adopted, without alteration. Subsequently a committee consisting of Mr. Latrobe, Mr. Evans, and Mr. Andersen, prepared a code of laws for the redress of injuries and for the regulation of property, together with a collection of legal forms, which have been in use up to the present time. The work of this committee was done by Mr. Evans.[1]

From the remarks of the President of the Historical Society after this paper had been read, it would appear that he and his colleagues in the Maryland Colonization movement, scarcely realized how consistent their action was with the ancient policy of this State, when the legal outcome of that policy, or the Ordinance of 1787, was thus unanimously adopted for the government of Maryland's own Colony in Liberia. Extremes meet in History as well as in Politics, and the present age could read a γνῶθι σαυτὸν, or 'know thyself,' in the records of the past. It was the custom of Greek colonists, setting out from Athens or Corinth, to take with them fire from the prytaneum of their native city, as emblematic of the political life, which they were to kindle upon some distant shore. Unlike the Greek colonists in political genius or capacity for freedom, but like them in the desire, common to all colonists, of improving their material condition, the emigrants to Liberia from this State gladly received

[1] See Memoir of Hugh Davey Evans, LL. D. By the Rev. Hall Harrison, M. A Hartford: printed by the Church Press Company, 1870, p. 159. For the two instruments first mentioned and for the code of laws, see Constitution and Laws of Maryland in Liberia. Baltimore, 1847. The Ordinance of 1787 is printed in the Land Laws of the United States, pp. 356-61, and also in the Old Journals of Congress, IV., pp 752-54.

from Maryland a system of equal laws. Who shall say that the Ordinance which was given them for their future government was wholly a borrowed fire, when the original Ordinance of 1787 is itself the historic product of Maryland's ancient zeal in founding a National Commonwealth.

APPENDIX.

I.

Washington's Land Speculations.

Perkins, in his Annals of the West, says that Washington was one of the foremost speculators in Western Lands after the close of the French and Indian War.[1] The Washington-Crawford Letters, recently edited in a most thorough and painstaking manner by C. W. Butterfield,[2] throw a strong light upon the enterprising nature of that man who was, assuredly, "first in peace" and who, even if the Revolution had not broken out, would have become the most active and representative spirit in American affairs. Washington's schemes for the colonization of his western lands by importing Germans from the Palatinate, are but an index of the direction his business pursuits might have taken, had not duty called him to command the Army and afterwards to head the State. But the influence of some of these early schemes may be traced in Washington's later measures of public policy and in his plans for the internal improvement of his country. Reserving, however, for another topic Washington's pioneer-efforts for opening up communication with the West, let us examine a few portions of the documentary evidence relating to his early land speculations. There is nothing to Washington's discredit in any of the Washington-Crawford Letters, but the following extracts may afford an interesting revelation of the worldly wisdom of the Father of his Country.

[1] Perkins, Annals of the West, p. 110.
[2] Washington-Crawford Letters concerning Western Lands. By C. W. Butterfield, Cincinnati: Robert Clarke & Co. 1877.

In Washington's letter to his friend Crawford,[1] dated September 21, 1767, the whole scheme of taking up the bounty lands is broached: "I offered in my last to join you in attempting to secure some of the most valuable lands in the King's part, which I think may be accomplished after awhile, notwithstanding the proclamation that restrains it at present, and prohibits the settling of them at all; for I can never look upon that proclamation in any other light (but this I say between ourselves) than as a temporary expedient to quiet the minds of the Indians. It must fall, of course, in a few years, especially when those Indians consent to our occupying the lands. Any person, therefore, who neglects the present opportunity of hunting out good lands, and in some measure marking and distinguishing them for his own, in order to keep others from settling them, will never regain it. If you will be at the trouble of seeking out the lands, I will take upon me the part of securing them, as soon as there is a possibility of doing it, and will, moreover, be at all the cost and charges of surveying and patenting the same. You shall then have such a reasonable proportion of the whole as we may fix upon at our first meeting; as I shall find it necessary, for the better furthering of the design, to let some of my friends be concerned in the scheme, who must also partake of the advantages.

By this time it may be easy for you to discover that my plan is to secure a good deal of land. You will consequently come in for a very handsome quantity; and as you will obtain it without

[1] William Crawford was a Virginia officer, who had served in the French and Indian War and who, in early life, had learned the art of surveying from Washington. Crawford removed to the back country in 1766 and settled at "Stewart's Crossing," on the Youghiogheny river. In the following year, Washington began a correspondence with his old friend which lasted until 1781. The particulars concerning Crawford's awful death by torture, at the hands of Indian savages, are given in "Crawford's Campaign against Sandusky in 1782," by C. W. Butterfield the editor of the above correspondence. See also Perkins, Annals of the West, pp. 246-7.

any costs or expenses, I hope you will be encouraged to begin the search in time. I would choose, if it were practicable, to get large tracts together; and it might be desirable to have them as near your settlement or Fort Pitt as they can be obtained of good quality, but not to neglect others at a greater distance, if fine bodies of it lie in one place. It may be worthy of your inquiry to find out how the Maryland back line will run,[1] and what is said about laying off Neale's grant. I will inquire particularly concerning the Ohio Company, that we may know what to apprehend from them. For my own part, I should have no objection to a grant of land upon the Ohio, a good way below Pittsburgh, but would first willingly secure some valuable tracts nearer at hand.

I recommend, that you keep this whole matter a secret, or trust it only to those in whom you can confide, and who can assist you in bringing it to bear by their discoveries of land. This advice proceeds from several very good reasons, and, in the first place, because I might be censured for the opinion I have given in respect to the King's proclamation, and then, if the scheme I am now proposing to you were known, it might give the alarm to others, and, by putting them upon a plan of the same nature, before we could lay a proper foundation for success ourselves, set the different interests clashing, and, probably, in the end, overturn the whole. All this may be avoided by a silent

[1] In regard to this point, Crawford replies September 29, 1767: "There is nothing to be feared from the Maryland back line, as it does not go over the mountain." (Washington-Crawford Letters, p. 10.) There had been a controversy, as we learn from Butterfield, between Maryland and Virginia, respecting the exact whereabouts of the said back line, for, in the Maryland charter, it was defined as a meridian, extending from the "first fountain of the Potomac" to the northern limits of *Terra Mariæ*. Maryland claimed the "first fountain of the *north* branch of the Potomac, as the starting-point of this meridian line, whereas Virginia insisted that the head of the *south* branch should be taken, for this would infringe, to a less degree, upon the latter's western territory." Crawford meant that, admitting Maryland's claim, the back line could not be run west of the mountains.

management, and the operation carried on by you under the guise of hunting game, which you may, I presume, effectually do, at the same time you are in pursuit of land. When this is fully discovered, advise me of it, and if there appears but a possibility of succeeding at any time hence, I will have the lands immediately surveyed, to keep others off, and leave the rest to time and my own assiduity.

If this letter should reach your hands before you set out, I should be glad to have your thoughts fully expressed on the plan here proposed, or as soon afterwards as convenient; for I am desirous of knowing in due time how you approve of the scheme. I am, etc."[1]

The following extract from Crawford's answer to the above letter shows that the project suited him:

"With regard to looking out land in the King's part, I shall heartily embrace your offer upon the terms you proposed; and as soon as I get out and have my affairs settled in regard to the first matters proposed, I shall set out in search of the latter. This may be done under a hunting scheme (which I intended before you wrote to me), and I had the same scheme in my head, but was at a loss how to accomplish it. I wanted a person in whom I could confide—one whose interest could answer my ends and his own. I have had several offers, but have not agreed to any; nor will I with any but yourself or whom you think proper."

In 1770, Washington crossed the Alleghanies and visited his friend Crawford, to see how the latter had succeeded in spying out the land. Washington's Journal of his tour to the Ohio is very interesting and contains the most minute details as to his impressions concerning the western country. Washington left his home at Mount Vernon on the fifth of October and arrived at Crawford's on the morning of the thirteenth. The following selections from his Journal will suffice to illustrate its tenor:

[1] Washington-Crawford Letters, pp. 3-5, or Sparks' Life and Writings of Washington, II., pp. 346-50.

13th.—Set out about sunrise; breakfasted at the Great Meadows — thirteen miles — and reached Captain Crawford's about five o'clock. The land from Gist's to Crawford's is very broken, though not mountainous; in spots exceedingly rich, and, in general, free from stones. Crawford's is very fine land; lying on the Youghiogheny, at a place commonly called Stewart's Crossing.

14th —At Captain Crawford's all day. Went to see a coal mine, not far from his house, on the banks of the river. The coal seemed to be of the very best kind, burning freely, and abundance of it.

15th.—Went to view some land, which Captain Crawford had taken up for me near the Youghiogheny, distant about twelve miles. This tract, which contains about one thousand six hundred acres, includes some as fine land as ever I saw, and a great deal of rich meadow. It is well watered, and has a valuable millseat, except that the stream is rather too slight, and, it is said, not constant more than seven or eight months in the year; but, on account of the fall, and other conveniences, no place can exceed it. In going to this land, I passed through two other tracts, which Captain Crawford had taken up for my brothers, Samuel and John. I intended to have visited the land, which Crawford had procured for Lund Washington, this day also, but, time falling short, I was obliged to postpone it. Night came on before I got back to Crawford's. . . . . The lands, which I passed over to-day, were generally hilly, and the growth chiefly white oak, but very good notwithstanding; and, what is extraordinary, and contrary to the property of all other lands I ever saw before, the hills are the richest land; the soil upon the sides and summits of them being as black as a coal, and the growth walnut and cherry. The flats are not so rich, and a good deal more mixed with stone.

[The lands above described were not taken up as bounty-lands, but under patents issued by the land-office of Pennsylvania. On the twentieth of October, Washington and Crawford, with a small party of white men and Indians, started on a trip down the Ohio;

to view the lands on that river and on the Great Kanawha, which Washington intended to secure for himself and his friends, under the proclamation of 1763, which authorized the granting of two hundred thousand acres of bounty-land to officers and soldiers who had served in the French and Indian War. The party reached the confluence of the Great Kanawha and Ohio rivers in twelve days from Pittsburgh.]

November 1st.—Before eight o'clock we set off with our canoe up the river, to discover what kind of lands lay upon the Kanawha. The land on both sides this river, just at the mouth, is very fine; but, on the east side, when you get towards the hills which I judge to be about six or seven hundred yards from the river, it appears to be wet, and better adapted for meadow than tillage. . . . . We judged we went up the Kanawha about ten miles to-day. . . . . .

2nd.—We proceeded up the river, with the canoe, about four miles farther, and then encamped, and went a hunting; killed five buffaloes, and wounded some others, three deer, &c. This country abounds in buffaloes and wild game of all kinds; and also in all kinds of wild fowl, there being in the bottoms a great many small, grassy ponds, or lakes, which are full of swans, geese, and ducks of different kinds. . . . . .

3d.—We set off down the river, on our return homeward, and encamped at the mouth. At the beginning of the bottom above the junction of the rivers, and at the mouth of the branch on the east side, I marked two maples, an elm, and hoop-wood tree, as a corner of the *soldiers' land* (if we can get it), intending to take all the bottom from hence to the rapids in the Great Bend into one survey. I also marked at the mouth of another run, lower down on the west side, at the lower end of the long bottom, an ash and hoop wood for the beginning of another of the soldiers' surveys, to extend up so as to include all the bottom in a body on the west side. In coming from our last encampment up the

Kanawha, I endeavored to take the courses and distances of the river by a pocket compass, and by guessing.

* * * * * * * *

December 1st.—Reached home, having been absent nine weeks and one day.[1]

The practical results of the above expedition appear in the following advertisement in the Maryland Journal and Baltimore Advertiser of August 20, 1773:

Mount Vernon in Virginia, *July* 15, 1773.

The subscriber having obtained patents for upwards of twenty thousand acres of land on the Ohio and Great Kanawha (ten thousand of which are situated on the banks of the first-mentioned river, between the mouths of the two Kanawhas, and the remainder on the Great Kanawha, or New River, from the mouth, or near it, upwards, in one continued survey) proposes to divide the same into any sized tenements that may be desired, and lease them upon moderate terms, allowing a reasonable number of years rent free, provided, within the space of two years from next October, three acres for every fifty contained in each lot, and proportionably for a lesser quantity, shall be cleared, fenced, and tilled; and that, by or before the time limited for the commencement of the first rent, five acres for every hundred, and proportionably, as above, shall be enclosed and laid down in good grass for meadow; and moreover, that at least fifty fruit trees for every like quantity of land shall be planted on the Premises. Any persons inclinable to settle on these lands may be more fully informed of the terms by applying to the subscriber, near Alexandria, or in his absence to Mr. Lund Washington; and would do well in communicating their intentions before the 1st of October next, in order that a sufficient number of lots may be laid off to answer the demand.

[1] Writings of Washington, II., pp. 516–34.

As these lands are among the first which have been surveyed in the part of the country they lie in, it is almost needless to premise that none can exceed them in luxuriance of soil, or convenience of situation, all of them lying upon the banks either of the Ohio and Kanawha, and abounding with fine fish and wild fowl of various kinds, as also in most excellent meadows, many of which (by the bountiful hand of nature) are, in their present state, almost fit for the scythe. From every part of these lands water carriage is now had to Fort Pitt, by an easy communication; and from Fort Pitt, up the Monongahela, to Redstone, vessels of convenient burthen, may and do pass continually; from whence by means of Cheat River, and other navigable branches of the Monongahela, it is thought the portage to Potowmack may, and will, be reduced within the compass of a few miles, to the great ease and convenience of the settlers in transporting the produce of their lands to market. To which may be added, that as patents have now actually passed the seals for the several tracts here offered to be leased, settlers on them may cultivate and enjoy the lands in peace and safety, notwithstanding the unsettled counsels respecting a new colony on the Ohio; and as no right money is to be paid for these lands, and quitrent of two shillings sterling a hundred, demandable some years hence only, it is highly presumable that they will always be held upon a more desirable footing than where both these are laid on with a very heavy hand. And it may not be amiss further to observe, that if the scheme for establishing a new government on the Ohio, in the manner talked of, should ever be effected, these must be among the most valuable lands in it, not only on account of the goodness of soil, and the other advantages above enumerated, but from their contiguity to the seat of government, which more than probable will be fixed at the mouth of the Great Kanawha.

GEORGE WASHINGTON.

These lands were patented by Lord Dunmore, Governor of Virginia, as we know from Washington's own statement to the

Reverend John Witherspoon, in a letter dated March 10, 1784,[1] in which he describes his western lands. From inferential evidence we are inclined to think that Washington obtained these patents before any general issue of land-grants had been made to the officers and soldiers. We know that Washington entered the claims of all those who applied to him for assistance, and that too as early as 1771,[2] but the general tenor of the Washington-Crawford Letters from that date up to January, 1774, indicates that no official grants had been issued.[3] In a letter to Crawford, dated September 25, 1773, Washington says, "I would recommend it to you to use dispatch, for, depend upon it, if it be once known that the Governor will grant patents for these lands, [below the Scioto,] the officers of Pennsylvania, Maryland, Carolina, etc., will flock there in shoals, and every valuable spot will be taken up contiguous to the river, on which the lands, unless it be where there are some peculiar properties, will always be most valuable."[4] I seems that Washington was mistaken in regard to the governor's intention, for, in a letter dated September 24, 1773, one day previous to the date of the above, Dunmore declares positively to Washington, that he does not mean to grant any patents on the western waters.[5] And yet, from the above advertisement, it is clear that Washington himself already held patents on western waters for upwards of twenty thousand acres.[6] It will be noticed, however, that Washington does not speak of these lands as patented under the proclamation of 1763, and yet, from allusions to them in his own letters, we know that they were thus obtained as bounty-lands,[7] and that Washington bought up the claims of his fellow-officers to a considerable extent. The

[1] Writings of Washington, XII., p. 264, or Washington-Crawford Letters, p. 77.
[2] Writings of Washington, II., p. 367.
[3] Washington-Crawford Letters, e. g. pp. 23, 25, 26, 29, 33, 35, 40.
[4] Washington-Crawford Letters, p. 33
[5] Writings of Washington, II., p. 379.
[6] Some light on this fact may, perhaps, be seen in the Writings of Washington, II., p. 367.
[7] Washington-Crawford Letters, p. 78.

following lettter to Crawford affords positive evidence on this point:

MOUNT VERNON, *September* 25, 1773.

"DEAR SIR:—I have heard (the truth of which, if you saw Lord Dunmore in his way to or from Pittsburgh, you possibly are better acquainted with than I am) that his Lordship will grant patents for lands lying below the Scioto, to the officers and soldiers who claim under the proclamation of October, 1763. If so, I think no time should be lost in having them surveyed, lest some new revolution should happen in our political system. I have, therefore, by this conveyance, written to Captain Bullitt, to desire he will have ten thousand acres surveyed for me; five thousand of which I am entitled to in my own right; the other five thousand, by purchase from a captain and lieutenant.

* * * * * * * *

Old David Wilper, who was an officer in our regiment, and has been with Bullitt running out land for himself and others, tells me that they have already discovered four salt springs in that country; three of which Captain Thompson has included within some surveys he has made; and the other, an exceedingly valuable one, upon the River Kentucky, is in some kind of dispute. I wish I could establish one of my surveys there; I would immediately turn it to an extensive public benefit, as well as private advantage. However, as four are already discovered, it is more than probable there are many others; and if you could come at the knowledge of them by means of the Indians, or otherwise, I would join you in taking them up in the name or names of some persons who have a right under the proclamation, and whose right we can be sure of buying, as it seems there is no other method of having lands granted; but this should be done with a good deal of circumspection and caution, till patents are obtained."[1]

* * * * * * * *

[1] Writings of Washington's, II., pp. 375–77, or Washington-Crawford Letters, pp. 29–31.

Exactly how much land Washington succeeded in getting patents for, it is difficult to say. From his letters to John Witherspoon and Presley Neville we know that he obtained, at least, 32,373 acres under the signature of Lord Dunmore.[1] Of this amount, ten thousand acres were doubtless secured about the beginning of the year 1774, when Lord Dunmore began to grant patents officially. In the preceding letter it will be noticed that Washington speaks of his desire to have that quantity of land surveyed. Reckoning the latter with the "upwards of twenty thousand acres" which Washington advertised in the Maryland Journal and Baltimore Advertiser, we can fairly account for the above 32,373 acres. It is not improbable that Washington owned at one time, even a larger amount of land than this, which he speaks of in the above letter to Presley Neville as still possessing in 1794.

At the office of the Johns Hopkins University there may be seen an original plot of survey, executed, probably, by Crawford, but, possibly, by Washington himself (for it contains some of his own handwriting), of 28,400 acres of land on the *Little Kanawha* river, patented in the name of Captain Stobo's heirs, of Captain Vanbraam, and of several other parties.[2] We have discovered

[1] Writings of Washington, XII., 264, 317, or Washington-Crawford Letters, pp 77, 82.

[2] This map of survey, formerly the property of Reverdy Johnson. Esq., was first recognized by President Gilman as containing some of George Washington's own handwriting, and, through the courtesy of Mr Johnson, this map, now framed, graces the President's office at the University. Professor J. E Hilgard, of the U. S. Coast survey, has called attention to the careful and accurate method of protraction employed in this plot of survey. It will be noticed that the course of the river is indicated by the straight lines of survey and not by curves.

The Publication Committee of the Maryland Historical Society, Messrs. Stockbridge, Cross, and Lee, have generously undertaken to present to our readers a *fac-simile* of this interesting relic. The words " Plot of the Survey on the Little Kanawha, 28,400 acres made in 1773," are written on the back of the original map, but have been photographed and inserted in the *fac-simile* for the sake of showing the whole.

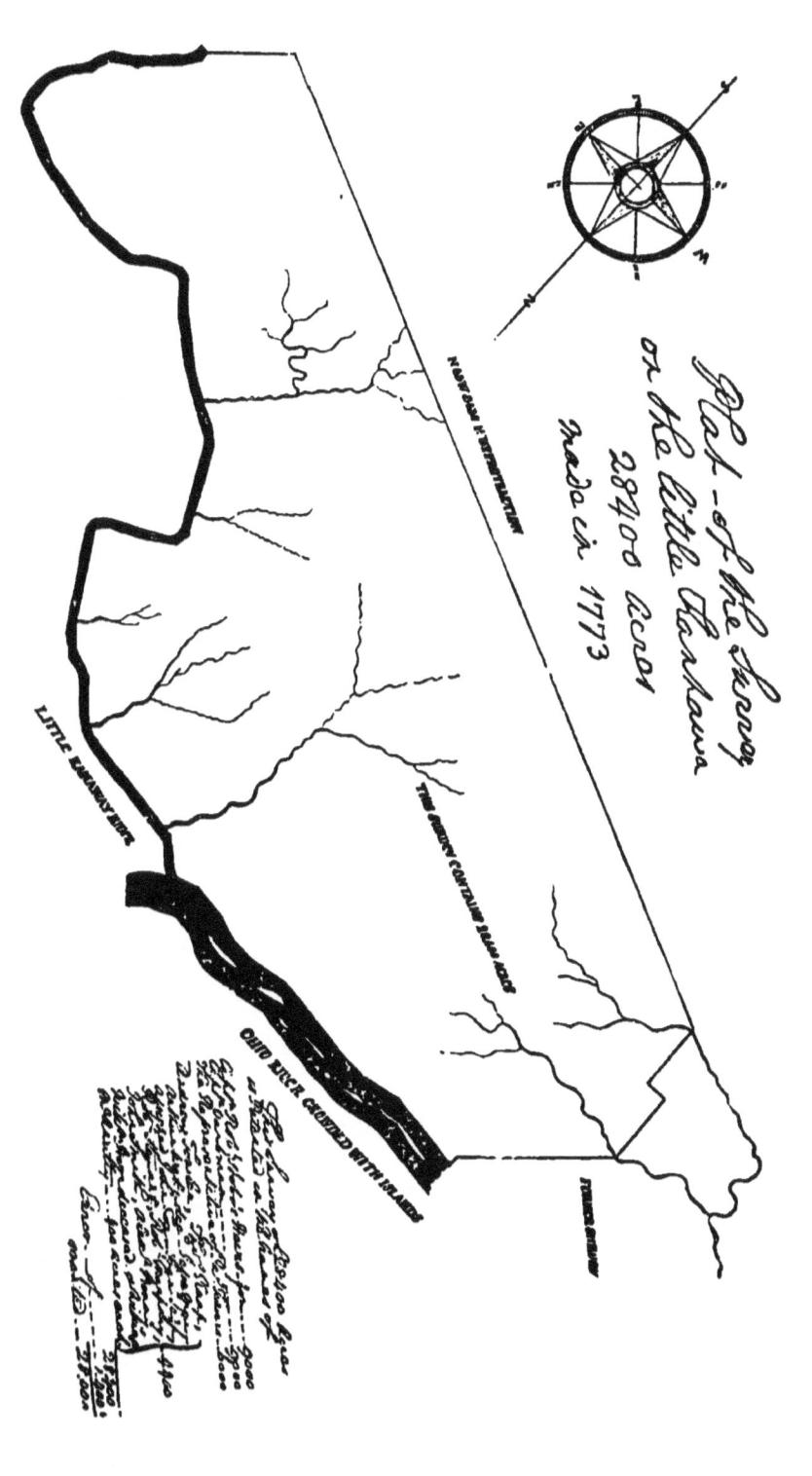

allusions to these two officers in the Writings of Washington (II., pp. 365, 368,) and know that they entered their claims, along with those of other friends and acquaintances of Washington, in the year 1771, but these two officers were out of the country and, as Washington complained, had not advanced their share of the expenses attending the surveys. It is highly probable that Captain Stobo (or his heirs) and Captain Vanbraam became tired of waiting for patents and sold out their claims to Washington, as did several gentlemen in this country. But we have more positive evidence that Washington owned property at the mouth of the Little Kanawha. And, in this connection, Lord Dunmore's interest in western lands must be slightly exposed. There is some obscurity attached to the royal governor's conduct and prudent delay in granting patents for the bounty lands, but there is no reason for suspecting Washington, for we know that he did his utmost to prevail upon Dunmore and his predecessor, Lord Botetourt, to hasten the grants.[1]

In the spring of 1773, we find Dunmore making arrangements with Washington for a trip over the mountains. The latter expresses his willingness to accompany the governor, about the first of July, "through any and every part of the western country" which Dunmore might think proper to visit. Crawford is recommended as a guide, because of "his superior knowledge of the country." Washington was prevented, however, by a family affliction,[2] from carrying out the project, but Dunmore went without him, and, very naturally, visited Crawford in his western home,

[1] See Letters to Lord Botetourt, the Earl of Dunmore, and George Mercer, 1770-1. Writings of Washington, II., pp. 355, 359, 365, 378. This correspondence ought to be published in every collection of documents relating to Western Lands. It would not be amiss in the Appendix to Butterfield's next edition, for these letters set Washington's character in a very clear light as regards honorable intentions by his fellow-officers.

[2] The death of Miss Custis, daughter of Mrs. Washington by her former marriage. See Sparks' Life and Writings of Washington, II., p. 378.

"the occasion being turned to profitable account," Butterfield thinks, " by both parties : by the Earl, in getting reliable information of desirable lands; by Crawford, in obtaining promises for patents for such as he had sought out and surveyed." These promises on Dunmore's part related to lands *at the mouth of the Little Kanawha.* This is evident from two passages in Crawford's letters to Washington : "In my last letter to you I wrote you that Lord Dunmore had promised me that in case the new government did not take place before he got home, he would patent these lands for me if I would send him the draft of the land I surveyed on the mouth of the Little Kanawha "[1] This passage is ambiguous, but it settles one point: the proposed draft of land was *at the mouth of the Little Kanawha.* The second passage, which is from a subsequent letter, clears up the ambiguity: " Lord Dunmore promised me most faithfully, that when I sent him the draft of land *on the Little Kanawha* that he would patent it *for me;* and in my letter to you I mentioned it, but have not heard anything from you relating to it."[2]

Now comes Washington's relation to the lands at the mouth of the Little Kanawha. The passage from Crawford, which was quoted first, is in immediate connection with the following offer: "Now, as my claim as an officer can not include the whole, if you will join as much of your officer's claim as will take all of the survey, you may depend I will make any equal division you may propose. I told Lord Dunmore the true state of the matter." The passage which was quoted in the second place, is immediately preceded by this statement: " He [Doctor Connolly, Lord Dunmore's agent] further told me that you had applied for my land as an officer, and could not obtain it without a certificate, or my being present; which puts me at a loss, in some measure, how to take it, especially as you have not written on that head." In this and in the succeeding sentence, above quoted, Crawford manifests

---

[1] Washington-Crawford Letters, p. 35.
[2] Washington-Crawford Letters, p. 40.

some anxiety in regard to securing patents on the lands at the mouth of the Little Kanawha, having heard nothing from Washington on that score.

And now comes the conclusion of the matter, as far as our evidence goes. In a letter to Washington, dated September 20, 1774, and, therefore, after patents had been issued in sufficient quantities to cover all purposes of speculation, Crawford says: "I have, I believe, as much land lying on the Little Kanawha as will make up the quantity you want, that I intended to lay your grants on; *but if you want it, you can have it,* and I will try to get other land for that purpose" [up river, as he proceeds to describe.] The sense of this passage is somewhat ambiguous, but, in the light of the foregoing facts, we think it must be interpreted as follows: Crawford had surveyed a large tract of land at the mouth of the Little Kanawha; he had offered to share it with Washington; the letter had applied for Crawford's patent and had secured certain grants in which he and Crawford were to have a joint interest, which grants Crawford had intended to lay upon the lands at the mouth of the Little Kanawha; but Washington, for some reason, desired to make up a quantity of land for himself, in one tract, and Crawford tells him that if he wants the whole tract at the mouth of the Little Kanawha, he can have it, and he himself will lay the warrants, in which he and Washington have a joint interest, upon a certain parcel of land "fifteen or twenty miles up that river, on the lower side, and [which] is already run out in tracts of about three thousand and some odd acres; others about twenty-five hundred acres; all well marked and bounded." This interpretation is borne out by the fact that Crawford's name does not appear in the list of patentees, which was written by Washington himself on the above mentioned map of survey, although the tract at the mouth of the Little Kanawha was certainly the one which Crawford originally surveyed for himself and which he desired to have Washington join him in securing. It is possible that the words "Former Survey," which are to be seen in the preceding plate, have reference to Crawford's first survey of the locality, a draft of which he sent to Lord Dunmore. It is highly probable that Washington bought up the claims of all the parties, in whose names the patents for the land at the mouth of the Little Kanawha were drawn, as the list itself shows, and secured the entire 28,400 acres for himself in one tract. Washington's practice of clapping purchased warrants upon Crawford's land-surveys is made evident by the following passage from one of Crawford's letters, dated March 6, 1775: "Inclosed you have two plats which you must fix warrants to yourself and the dates also of the warrants."[1] Whether Crawford had obtained from Lord Dunmore, before that date, any regular commission as surveyor for a district on the Ohio, is not clear. We know, however, that Lord Dunmore promised to serve Crawford in that way if it should be in his power,[2] and Crawford wrote to Washington, December 29, 1773, concerning this very matter: "If you can do any thing for me, pray do; as it will then be in my power to be of service to you, and myself too, and our friends."[3] A few months previous to the above date, Washington had procured for Crawford the position of surveyor for the Ohio Land Company.[4] Crawford seems to have been a very enterprising character. If *he* could have managed the patenting of the bounty-lands, he would doubtless have served himself, Washington, and "our friends" far more effectually than did Lord Dunmore.[5] In a

[1] Washington-Crawford Letters, p. 59. As Washington did not go west in 1773, it is probable that he affixed the names of Stobo, Vanbraam, and the rest, to a plot that Crawford had sent him.
[2] Washington-Crawford Letters, pp. 39, 40.
[3] Washington-Crawford Letters, p. 39.
[4] Washington-Crawford Letters, p. 33.
[5] There are strong reasons for believing that Lord Dunmore and his Council were materially interested not only in restraining the soldier's grants, but also in furthering the claims of certain land companies in which they had stock. Washington ascribes the backwardness of this Honorable Board, in recognizing the soldiers' claims, to "other causes" than mere lukewarmness. (See Writings of Washington, II., p. 365.)

letter to Wahington dated November 12, 1773, Crawford hints at taking up the entire two hundred thousand acres: "I wrote you," he says, "relating to the upper survey on the Great Kanawha. I think you have not apprehended me in what I wanted. *There is the full quantity of land of two hundred thousand acres, and six hundred over and above.*" Butterfield says that Crawford's meaning at this point is not clear. At least the allusion to the two hundred thousand acres must have conveyed a tolerably clear concept to the speculative mind of Washington.

If Washington really owned at one time, the above 28,400 acres in addition to the 32,373 acres which we have previously accounted for, this amount, together with his 10,000 acres of unpatented surveys, would make a sum total of 70,773 acres of western land, which he aspired to control. Considering the fact that his own claim as an officer was for but five thousand acres and that only two hundred thousand could possibly be granted to the officers and soldiers, it would certainly appear as though Washington meant to secure the lion's share, which, considering the circumstances and Lord Dunmore's conduct, no one could truly begrudge that enterprising man who prevented Dunmore and his colleagues from buying up all the claims. Washington needs no defence but his own manly and straightforward statements to his friend George Mercer, concerning his efforts to

It is stated, as a notorious fact, in the famous Virginia Remonstrance (see Hening, Virginia Statutes at Large, X , p. 558,) that Lord Dunmore was in league with "men of great influence in some of the neighboring states," for the purpose of securing, under cover of purchase from the Indians, large tracts of country between the Ohio and Mississippi. By the allusion to "neighboring states," Maryland is aimed at, for Virginians usually ascribed Maryland's zeal for the public good to the interested motives of individuals. Such hints recoil, however, upon Virginia without damage to Maryland, for the policy of *all* the smaller states and the sturdy persistance. as well as the united and thoroughly consistent action of Maryland, are not to be explained from the standpoint of individual interest.

secure the bounty-lands for the officers and soldiers. "The unequal interest and dispersed situation of the claimants," he says, "make a regular coöperation difficult. An undertaking of this kind cannot be conducted without a good deal of expense and trouble; and the doubt of obtaining the lands, after the utmost efforts, is such as to discourage the larger part of the claimants from lending assistance, *whilst a few are obliged to wade through every difficulty, or relinquish every hope.* . . . . What inducements have men to explore uninhabited wilds, but the prospect of getting good lands? Would any man waste his time, expose his fortune, nay, life, in such a search, if he was to share the good and the bad with those that come after him? Surely not."[1]

It is necessary to add, moreover, in closing this long disquisition on Washington's Land Speculations, which, after all, is not without its purpose in our exposition of the material basis of the American Union, that the Father of his Country did not realize as much as he had expected from his investment of time and money. His experience with Western Land seems to have been like that of many speculators of our own day. In a letter to Presley Neville, in 1794, he says: "From a long experience of many years, I have found distant property in land more pregnant of perplexities than profit. I have therefore resolved to sell all I hold on the Western waters, if I can obtain the prices which I conceive their quality, their situation, and other advantages, would authorize me to expect." In this letter, Washington estimates some of his land at six dollars per acre, and other portions at four dollars. He says he once sold his 32,373 acres, on the Great Kanawha and Ohio rivers, for sixty-five thousand French crowns to "a French gentleman, who was very competent to the payment at the time the contract was made; but, getting a little embarrassed in his finances by the revolution in his country, by mutual agreement the bargain was cancelled." Washington

[1] Writings of Washington, II., pp. 365, 366.

declares also that he has lately been negotiating for the sale of his western property at three and one third dollars per acre.[1] But the lands on the Great Kanawha alone were afterwards sold, conditionally, for two hundred thousand dollars, as we learn from the schedule of property appended to Washington's will. "If the terms of that sale are not complied with," Washington adds in a foot-note, "they [these lands] will command considerably more " A good idea of the vast extent of Washington's investments in land may be obtained from an examination of this schedule,[2] the details of which we have somewhat abridged. The schedule does not include the Mount Vernon estates which embraced six thousand acres, or the tracts on Little Hunting Creek and Four Mile Run, which, together, formed three thousand two hundred and twenty-seven acres; this home-property, comprising in all 9,227 acres, was reserved in family estates for Bushrod Washington and others. The estimates of the value of the following parcels were made by Washington himself, in 1799, and his heirs were directed to sell off this larger portion of his landed property.

LANDS IN VIRGINIA.

	Acres.	Value.
Loudoun County, Difficult Run,	300	$ 6,666
Loudoun and Fauquier,	3,366	31,890
Berkeley,	22,236	44,720
Frederic,	571	11,420
Hampshire,	240	3,600
Gloucester,	400	3,600
Nansemond, near Suffolk,	373	2,984
Great Dismal Swamp, dividend thereof,	[?]	20,000
Carried forward,	27,486	$124,880

[1] Writings of Washington, XII., 318 or Appendix to the Washington-Crawford Letters, p. 62.
[2] Writings of Washington, I., pp. 581-2.

	Acres.	Value.
Brought forward,	27,486	$124,880

LANDS ON THE OHIO.

Round Bottom,	587	
Little Kanawha,	2,314	
Sixteen miles lower down,	2,448	
Opposite Big Bent,	4,395	
	9,744	$97,440

LANDS ON THE GREAT KANAWHA.

Near the mouth, west,	10,990	
East side, above,	7,276	
Mouth of Cole River,	2,000	
Opposite thereto,	2,950	
Burning Spring,	125	
	23,341	$200,000

LANDS IN MARYLAND.

Charles County,	600	3,600
Montgomery,	519	6,228
	1,119	$ 9,828

LANDS IN PENNSYLVANIA.

Great Meadows,	234	1,404

LANDS IN NEW YORK.

Mohawk River,	1,000	6,000

LANDS IN NORTHWEST TERRITORY.

On Little Miami,	3,051	15,255
Carried forward,	65,975	$454,807

	Acres.	Value.
Brought forward	65,975	$454,807

LANDS IN KENTUCKY.

	Acres.	Value.
Rough Creek,	5,000	10,000
Total,	70,975	$464,807
LOTS IN WASHINGTON,		19,132
" " ALEXANDRIA,		4,000
" " WINCHESTER,		400
		$488,339

Thus, to say nothing of the Mount Vernon estates, of the lands that Washington had previously disposed of in the Mohawk valley,[1] and elsewhere, of the 28,400 acres *at the mouth* of the Little Kanawha,[2] of the 10,000 acres of unpatented surveys lost by the Revolution, or of Washington's share in the Great Dismal Swamp, thus we see, that he actually owned, in 1799, over 70,000 acres of land, which he had originally secured for speculative purposes alone.

These facts concerning the vast extent of Washington's landed interests are now for the first time brought into systematic shape and historic connection. They reveal the practical and intensely American spirit of the Father of our Country. It does not detract from Washington's true greatness for the world to know this material side of his character. On the contrary, it only exalts that heroic spirit which, in disaster, never faltered, and which, in success, would have no reward. To be sure, it brings Washington nearer the level of humanity to know that he was endowed with the passions common to men, and that he was as diligent in business as he was fervent in his devotion to country. It may seem less ideal to view Washington as a man rather than as a

---

[1] Writings of Washington, I, p. 584.

[2] The claims of Stobo and Vanbraam were really purchased by Washington's London agent, as we have just ascertained from a note in Irving's Life of Washington, I., p. 369.

hero or statesman, but history deals with men and, before all things, with human realties. Man lives for himself, as well as in and for the State, and the distinction of individual from patriotic motives is one of the necessary tasks of historical investigation.

II.

Washington's Public Spirit in Opening a Channel of Trade between East and West.

Public spirit and private enterprise are the leading traits of the American people. This dualism of character constitutes the healthful vigor of our state-life. The coëxistence in George Washington of the most earnest zeal for the public good and of the most active spirit of business enterprise, is but the prototype of the life of our nation, for, as a distinguished jurist and political philosopher has well said, DER STAT IST DER MANN IM GROSSEN (*l'état c'est l'homme*).[1] A proper balance between public and individual interests is the great problem of self government, but public good, and not the individual will, must be the determining power in this adjustment. When the commonwealth rises paramount and supreme over such selfish strivings as those recorded in the history of the land-controversy, then does the true soul of State assert its sovereign will. Necessity is the supreme law of nations as well as of men, and it springs, sometimes, full-armed into being from the most material of human interests. The real essence of Political Sovereignty we cannot explain. As Shakespeare says:

> "There is a mystery
> in the soul of State,
> Which hath an operation more divine
> Than breath or pen can give expressure to."[2]

[1] J. C. Bluntschli: Lehre vom Modernen Stat, I., p. 25. Bluntschli is professor of public and international law at Heidelberg and *président de l'Institut de droit international*, which holds its yearly meetings in Belgium.

[2] Troilus and Cressida, Act III., Scene 3.

Political Sovereignty has its prototype, however, in the public spirit and patriotism of the individual. Who can account for the generous nature of American citizens, or for that heroic spirit which sometimes creates whole armies of men, who are ready to sacrifice all their individual interests for some great cause? Americans are said to be the most practical people in the world, and they probably are. We even call the State "a machine," although it may be doubted if any but Englishmen believe this political doctrine. Americans are far too practical to offer up their lives for the sake of a machine, or to drag a political juggernaut for the privilege of being crushed by its wheels. Public good, however, takes precedence of individual happiness. The State is surely as noble as the patriotism which leads men to die for it. Although *interest* is, without doubt, the material basis of political society, as it is of human action, yet there is an interest in Man, as well as in the State, which transcends self-interest and all personal or material aims. It seldom finds perfect expression, either in Man or in the State, but it is the glory of human nature that self-interest sometimes *does* find a sovereign complement in a spirit of self-sacrifice for the common good and for the welfare of others. Such was the self-sacrificing devotion of George Washington, when, at the outbreak of the Revolution, he received from Congress the commission of Commander-in-Chief of the American forces, and, standing in his place as member of the House from Virginia, uttered those memorable words: "I will enter upon the momentous duty, and exert every power I possess for the support of the glorious cause. But lest some unlucky event should happen, unfavorable to my reputation, I beg it may be remembered by every gentleman in the room, that I this day declare, with the utmost sincerity, I do not think myself equal to the command I am honored with. As to pay, sir, I beg leave to assure the Congress that, as no pecuniary consideration could have tempted me to accept this arduous employment, at the expense of my domestic ease and happiness, I do not wish to make any profit from it. I will keep an exact account of my expenses. These I doubt not they will discharge, and that is all I desire."[1]

Washington's patriotism in the defense of American liberty needs no eulogy. On the twenty-third of December, 1783, he tendered his resignation to Congress, then in session at Annapolis, in a speech which has an abiding fame, as that of the American Cincinnatus. These are his concluding words: "Having now finished the work assigned me, I retire from the great theatre of action, and, bidding an affectionate farewell to this august body under whose orders I have so long acted, I here offer my commission, and take leave of all the employments of public life."[2]

But Washington's activity in the service of this country had but just begun. We refer not to his subsequent career as President of these United States, after the adoption of the present Constitution in 1788, but to his public spirit in opening up the Great West to trade and commerce, and in laying the basis for our nation's policy in the matter of internal improvements. This is a chapter in Washington's life that is not so well known. Materials for this subject were first collected by Mr. Andrew Stewart, member of Congress from Pennsylvania, in a Report on the "Chesapeake and Ohio Canal," in 1826.[3] Some, but not all, of the Washington-documents pertaining to this matter were republished by Sparks, in his edition of the Writings of Washington. Mr. John Pickell, formerly one of the Directors of the Chesapeake and Ohio Canal Company, has worked over this material and compiled fresh facts from official sources in a valuable monograph called, "A new chapter in the Early Life of Washington in connection with the narrative history of the Potomac Company."[4]

---

[1] Writings of Washington, III., p. 1. Compare with letter to Mrs. Washington, III , pp. 2–3.

[2] Writings of Washington, VIII., p. 505.

[3] Reports of Committees of the House of Representatives, First Session, Nineteenth Congress. Report No. 228.

[4] New York: D. Appleton & Co., 1856.

The connection of George Washington with schemes for opening communication between the Atlantic States and the Great West was broken by the Revolution. There is a report in George Washington's handwriting, dated as far back as 1754, stating the difficulties to be overcome in rendering the Potomac navigable.[1] This report was made by Washington on his return from a trip across the Alleghanies, as messenger from Governor Dinwiddie to the commandant of the French forces on the Ohio. Washington went up the Potomac to Will's creek,[2] or Fort Cumberland, and over the Alleghanies by the route which was afterwards taken by the unfortunate Braddock, in his expedition against the French and Indians, and which became known as Braddock's Road.[3] A route was afterwards mapped out by Washington, from Cumberland over the mountains to the Youghiogheny river, which was destined to become the great avenue of travel and western migration. The construction of the Cumberland turnpike was a national work.[4] Indeed it was called the *National Road*, and it must be regarded as one of the direct results of that policy of internal improvement, which, as we shall see, originated with Washington. The historic outcome of the Cumberland turnpike is, however, the Connellsville line, from Pittsburgh to Cumberland, of the Baltimore and Ohio Railroad.

The spirit of history is the self-knowledge of the Present concerning its process of development from the Past. There must be some germ for historical as well as for natural evolution. The Potomac scheme of George Washington contained, in germ, about all that the present generation could reasonably demand. In a

[1] Stewart's Report, p. 1. Sparks has not reprinted this document.
[2] Washington's journal of a tour over the Alleghany Mountains, Writings, II., p. 432.
[3] This route was originally discovered by Indians in the the employ of Virginia and Pennsylvania traders. It was first opened by the Ohio Company in 1753. See Writings of Washington, II., p. 302
[4] The Cumberland Road was completed to Wheeling in 1825 at a cost of $1,700 000. Hildreth, History of the United States, 1750-1820, III., p. 699.

letter to Thomas Johnson,[1] the first state-governor of Maryland, dated July 20, 1770, Washington suggests that the project of opening up the Potomac be "recommended to the public notice upon *a more enlarged plan*" [i. e. passage to Cumberland and connection, by portage, with Ohio waters] "*as a means of becoming the channel of conveyance of the extensive and valuable trade of a rising empire.*[2]

[1] Thomas Johnson, of Maryland, was the man who, in 1775, nominated George Washington for the office of Commander-in-Chief of the American army. See Writings of Washington, III., p. 480 He was one of the committee of correspondence for Maryland, in 1775, Samuel Chase, Charles Carroll of Carrollton, Charles Carroll, barrister, and William Paca, being among his colleagues. He was delegate to Congress from 1775–77, and Governor of Maryland from 1777–79. Lanman, in his Biographical Annals of the Civil Government of the United States, is surely mistaken in saying that Johnson left Congress to raise a small army with which, as commander, he went to the assistance of Washington *in New England*. Governor Johnson called out extra militia in 1777 "to defend our liberties," but Washington left New England and retreated from Long Island in 1776, the Maryland Line covering the retreat, after having saved Putnam's troops from destruction by charging six times, with the bayonet, upon the left wing of the British army and by the sacrifice of five devoted companies, of whom Washington said: "My God! what brave men must I this day lose!" Colonel Smallwood was the commander of these brave young men from Baltimore, although he did not take part in the engagement, being "absent on duty in New York." (Bancroft, IX., p. 88.) But though Governor Johnson did not go to Washington's relief, these two were ever the warmest friends, and, after the Revolution, often visited each other, now at Rose Hill, near Frederick, and now at Mount Vernon. Johnson was Justice of the Supreme Court of the United States from 1791–93, and, when Jefferson left the Cabinet, was invited by Washington to become Secretary of State, but declined. John Adams was once asked how it was that so many Southern men took part in the Revolution, and he replied, that, if it hadn't been for such men as Richard Henry Lee, Thomas Jefferson, Samuel Chase, and Thomas Johnson, there never would have been any Revolution. See Lanman's Biographical Annals, "Thomas Johnson."

[2] This letter to Thomas Johnson of Maryland is not to be found in Sparks' collection of the Writings of Washington but in Stewart's Report, pp. 27-29. The idea advanced is of colossal import and only the present generation can realize its full significance.

Here is the *bahnbrechende Idee*, whose resistless strength has opened up the vistas of our inland commerce, and whose colossal proportions are now revealed, not only in the Baltimore and Ohio, which is the direct historic outgrowth of the Potomac scheme, but in the whole system of communication between East and West. It is a surprising fact that George Washington not only first mapped out and recommended that line, which is now in very truth, "*becoming* the channel of conveyance of the extensive and valuable trade of a rising empire," but was also the first to predict the commercial success of that route through the Mohawk valley, which was afterwards taken by the Erie Canal and the New York Central Rail Road. He not only predicted the accomplishment of this line of communication with the West, but he actually explored it in person. Before he had repaired to Annapolis to resign his commission, and even before the terms of peace with Great Britain had been definitely arranged, Washington was again turning his attention to the scheme of opening up the West to trade and commerce. He left his camp at Newburgh on the Hudson, and made, on horseback, an exploring expedition of nearly three weeks' duration through the State of New York. In a letter to the Marquis of Chastelleux, he gives an account of his trip: "I have lately made," he says, "a tour through the lakes George and Champlain, as far as Crown Point: then returning to Schenectady, I proceeded up the Mohawk river to Fort Schuyler; crossed over the Wood creek which empties into the Oneida lake, and affords the water communication with Ontario. I then traversed the country to the head of the Eastern branch of the Susquehannah, and viewed the lake Otswego, and the portage between that lake and the Mohawk river, at Conajoharie. Prompted by these actual observations, I could not help taking a more contemplative and extensive view of the vast inland navigation of these United States, and could not but be struck with the immense diffusion and importance of it; and with the goodness of that Providence which has dealt his favors to us with so profuse a hand. Would to God we may have wisdom enough to improve them! I shall not rest contented until I have explored the Western country, and traversed those lines (or a great part of them) which have given bounds to a new empire."[1]

After resigning his commission at Annapolis, Washington returned to Mount Vernon where he arrived the day before Christmas, 1783. "The scene is at last closed," he writes, four days afterwards, to Governor Clinton, of New York, who had accompanied Washington in his recent explorations, "I feel myself eased of a load of public care. I hope to spend the remainder of my days in cultivating the affections of good men, and in the practice of the domestic virtues."[2] But how impossible it was for Washington to continue a mere private citizen, on the banks of the Potomac, solacing himself with the tranquil enjoyments of home life, as he had promised himself and his friends, is evinced by a letter to Thomas Jefferson, the following spring, in which he returns with fresh zeal to the project of national improvement. "How far, upon mature consideration," he says, "I may depart from the resolution I had formed, of living perfectly at my ease, exempt from every kind of responsibility, it is more than I can at present absolutely determine. . . . . The trouble, if my situation at the time would permit me, to engage in a work of this sort [the Potomac scheme] would be set at nought; and the immense advantages, which this country would derive from the measure, would be no small stimulus to the undertaking, if that undertaking could be made to comport with those ideas, and that line of conduct, with which I meant to glide gently down the current of life, and it did not interfere with any other plan I might have in contemplation."[3] The connection of this revival of public spirit with those recent explorations, with

---

[1] Stewart's Report, p. 2. Marshall's Life of Washington, V., p. 9.
[2] Writings of Washington, IX., p. 1.
[3] Writings of Washington, IX., p. 32.

Governor Clinton,[1] in the Mohawk valley is shown by this allusion: "I know the Yorkers will delay no time to remove every obstacle in the way of the *other* communication, so soon as the posts of Oswego and Niagara are surrendered." Washington requests, moreover, that Jefferson should confer with Thomas Johnson, formerly governor of Maryland, on this subject, as he had been a warm promoter of the Potomac scheme before the Revolution broke out.

In the light of these suggestions, we are not surprised to find Washington soon actively engaged in furthering the enterprise for which, ten years before, he had enlisted the legislative sympathies of Virginia and had secured the hearty coöperation of Mr. Johnson of Maryland. Washington started on another tour to the west on the first of September, 1784, and was absent from home a little more than a month. His tour westward was less extensive than he had contemplated,[2] for the Indians were still dangerous, but he managed to traverse six hundred and eighty miles on horseback, and took careful notes in his journal of all conversations with the settlers and other persons who were acquainted with the facilities for communication between east and west. There is an interesting fac-simile, in Stewart's Report, of a map of the country between the waters of the Potomac and those of the Youghiogheny and Monongahela rivers, as sketched

---

[1] It is highly characteristic of these two public spirits that they took occasion to secure together 6,000 acres of land on the Mohawk river, (Montgomery County.) See Washington's will, Sparks, I., p. 584, note (o). From a letter to Clinton of November 25, 1784, it would appear that the two friends had talked of buying up Saratoga Springs! Writings of Washington, IX., p. 70.

[2] Washington had intended to make a trip down the Ohio as far as the Great Kanawha, for the purpose of inspecting his lands in that region. We must not lose sight of Washington's business nature. "I am not going to explore the country, nor am I in search of fresh lands, but to secure what I have," writes he to Dr. Craik, July 10, 1784. But in this statement, Washington was not quite just towards his own motives, as events show.

by Washington in 1784. A new route of portage, which he designates from Cumberland to the Youghiogheny, does not deviate materially from the line afterwards taken by the Great National Road. Washington employed men at his own expense to explore the different ways of communication, and, from their detailed reports[1] and his own experience, he arrived at the conclusion that there were two practicable routes[2] to the Ohio valley, the one over the mountains from Cumberland, *via* Wills Creek and Pennsylvania, which is now the Connellsville branch of the Baltimore and Ohio, or the so-called Pittsburgh, Washington, and Baltimore railroad, and the other through the mountains from Cumberland, along the upper Potomac, which is now the grand route to Wheeling and Parkersburgh, from which points the Baltimore and Ohio stretches its Briarean arms to the Lakes and to the Father of Waters.

But we seek the beginning of all this. The first results of Washington's tour of exploration appear in a letter to Benjamin Harrison, Governor of Virginia, dated the tenth of October, 1784, which we must regard as a fresh *Ausgangspunkt* and the real historic beginning of the Potomac enterprise. With prophetic instinct, Washington seemed to realize the greatness of his scheme. "I shall take the liberty now, my dear Sir, to suggest a matter, which would (if I am not too short-sighted a politician) mark your administration as an important era in the annals of this country if it should be recommended by you and adopted by the Assembly."[3] Washington then proceeds to support by facts what had long been his "decided opinion," that the shortest and

---

[1] Two of these reports are reprinted by Stewart and are not to be found in Sparks' collection of Letters to Washington.

[2] See report of the Maryland and Virginia commissioners in regard to extending the navigation of the Potomac and constructing two roads to the west, one through Pennsylvania, the other " wholly through Virginia and Maryland," to Cheat river. Pickell, p. 45. Compare Washington's letter to Madison, December 28, 1784. Stewart's Report, p. 85.

[3] Writings of Washington, IX., p. 58.

least expensive route to the West was by way of the Potomac. He takes Detroit as the supposed point of departure of trade from the northwest territory, and shows that the Potomac connection is nearer tide-water than the St. Lawrence, by one hundred and sixty-eight miles, and nearer the West than the Hudson at Albany, by one hundred and seventy-six miles. Washington's calculation of distances, by way of Fort Pitt, a list which was appended to the above letter, is not reprinted in Sparks, but was copied by Stewart from the orignal manuscript, loaned him by General Mason of Virginia.[1]

"Distances from Detroit to the several Atlantic sea ports.

From Detroit, by the route through Fort Pitt and Fort Cumberland:—

	Miles.
To Alexandria, (or Washington City,)	607
" Richmond,	840
" Philadelphia,	745
" Albany,	943
" New York,	1103[2]"

Washington points out to governor Harrison the prospect of Pennsylvania's opening up communication with Pittsburgh by way of the Susquehanna and Toby's Creek and then cutting a canal between the former and the Schuylkill river. He says "a people who are possessed of the spirit of commerce, who see and who will pursue their advantages, may achieve almost anything." That New York also would join in "*smoothing the roads and paving the ways for the trade of the western world,*" Washington clearly foresaw. On this point, he says, "no person, who knows

[1] See Stewart's Report, p. 2, or Pickell's History of the Potomac Company, p. 174.
[2] Pittsburgh, the head of steamboat navigation on the Ohio, is now actually distant from New York by French Creek, Lake Erie, and the Erie Canal, 784 miles. From Pittsburgh to Washington, by the Chesapeake and Ohio Canal, it is 346 miles.

the temper, genius, and policy of those people as well as I do, can harbor the smallest doubt."[1] Washington's language seems almost prophetic.

The political importance of establishing commercial connections with the West seems to have impressed Washington most profoundly. He reminds Harrison how "the flanks and rear of the United States are possessed by other powers, and formidable ones too" [Spain and England.] He dwells upon the necessity of cementing all parts of the Union together by common interests. The Western States stand now, he says "upon a pivot." A touch would turn them. The stream of commerce would glide gently down the Mississippi unless shorter and easier channels were made for it to the Atlantic seaports. Washington urges that commissioners be appointed to make a careful survey of the Potomac and James rivers to their respective sources and that a complete map of the whole country intervening between the seaboard, the Ohio waters, and the Great Lakes, be presented to the public. "These things being done," he says, "I shall be mistaken if prejudice does not yield to facts, jealousy to candor, and, finally, if reason and nature, thus aided, do not dictate what is right and proper to be done."

[1] While advocating the Potomac route to a citizen of Maryland, Washington declares with patriotic fervor: "I am not for discouraging the exertions of any state to draw the commerce of the western country to its seaports. The more communications we open to it, the closer we bind that rising world (for, indeed, it may be so called) to our interests, and the greater strength we shall acquire by it." (See Marshall's Life of Washington, V., p. 12.)

To a member of Congress he expresses himself even more positively: "For my own part, I wish sincerely every door of that country [the West] may be set wide open, and the commercial intercourse with it rendered as free and easy as possible. This, in my opinion, is the *best*, if not the *only cement*, that can bind these People to us for any length of time; and we shall be deficient in foresight and wisdom if we neglect the means of effecting it."

Stewart's Report, p. 7. Neither of these passages are to be found in Sparks' collection of the Writings of Washington.

This letter to governor Harrison was brought before the legislature of Virginia, and public spirit in favor of the Potomac scheme was soon awakened. It became necessary to secure the coöperation of Maryland and a perfect harmony of legislative action on the part of both states in chartering the proposed company. A deputation, consisting of General Washington, General Gates, and Colonel Blackburn, was accordingly sent by the Virginia legislature to Annapolis, in December 1784, where they were received with distinguished honors A delegation was straightway appointed by the legislature of Maryland to confer with the gentlemen from Virginia. Among the Maryland commissioners was Charles Carroll of Carrollton, the man who was destined to see the historic development of that "enlarged plan," which Washington had so early recommended to Thomas Johnson of Maryland, for, on the fourth of July, 1828, this Nestor of American patriots, who had outlived all other signers of the Declaration of Independence, laid the first stone of the Baltimore and Ohio railroad.[1]

It is not our purpose to write another history of the Potomac Company. That work has been done by Pickell Our object is to show the public spirit and pioneer influence of George Washington in opening a channel of trade between East and West. His suggestions were adopted by the commissioners; his views were embodied in their report to the legislatures of Maryland and Virginia; and this report was the basis of all subsequent legislative action in regard to the proposed enterprise. Washington, moreover, introduced his plan to the notice of Congress, on account of its political bearing in turning the channels of trade

---

[1] Charles Carroll of Carrollton was over ninety years old at the time the Baltimore and Ohio was founded. His speech to a friend on that occasion was not unworthy the beginning of railroad enterprise in this country: "I consider this among the most important acts of my life, second only to my signing the Declaration of Independence, if even it be second to that." History and Description of the Baltimore and Ohio Railroad. By a Citizen of Baltimore. 1853, p. 20.

away from Spanish and British influence. "Extend the navigation of the eastern waters;" he writes to a member of Congress, "communicate them as near as possible with those which run westward—open those to the Ohio; open also such as extend from the Ohio toward Lake Erie, and we shall not only draw the produce of the western settlers, but the peltry and the fur-trade of the lakes to our ports; thus adding an immense increase to our exports, and *binding these people to us by a chain which can never be broken* "[1] This was the first suggestion to Congress of that policy of internal improvements, which, from the beginning of the National Road, in 1806, was followed up with considerable zeal, until General Jackson vetoed the Maysville Road, in 1829. The policy of Exploration and National Surveys, which our government still adheres to, was likewise suggested by George Washington, and that too in connection with the Potomac scheme. [2]

The public spirit of George Washington is strikingly manifest, not only in these pioneer efforts for the good of our nation, but in a project which is so nearly connected with the Potomac enterprise, that we must not pass it by, although the limits of this paper will not allow us a special treatment of the subject. Before the organization of the Potomac Company, of which George Washington became the first president in 1785, continuing in office until 1788,[3] when he was elected president of the United States, the legislature of Virginia passed an act vesting George Washington with one hundred and fifty shares in the proposed companies for extending the navigation of the Potomac and James

[1] Marshall's Life of Washington, V., p. 14. It is a mistake to suppose that Washington did not appreciate the importance of the Mississippi to the United States, and the true interests of the country in obtaining a free navigation of that river. He saw that this would come in good time. See Letter to R H Lee, July 19, 1787.

[2] See letter to Richard Henry Lee, President of Congress, 1784. Writings of Washington, IX., p. 80.

[3] The second president of the Potomac Company was Thomas Johnson of Maryland, the man to whom Washington addressed the letter of July 20, 1770, suggesting "an enlarged plan" for the Potomac enterprise.

rivers. This was done by the State of Virginia, through their representatives, who desired to testify "their sense of the unexampled merits of George Washington," and to make those great works for national improvement which were to be monuments to his glory, at the same time "monuments also of the gratitude of his country."

Washington, although deeply sensible of the honor his countrymen had shown him, felt himself much embarrassed by this substantial token of their good will and affection, and consequently declined their offer, for he wished, he said, to have his future actions "free and independent as the air." In a letter to Benjamin Harrison, Governor of Virginia, Washington, after a graceful tribute to the generosity of his native state, thus declares his position: "Not content with the bare consciousness of my having, in all this navigation business, acted upon the clearest conviction of the political importance of the measure, I would wish that every individual who may hear that it was a favorite plan of mine, may know, also, that I had no other motive for promoting it, than the advantage of which I conceived it would be productive to the Union, and to this State in particular, by cementing the eastern and western territory together. . . . .

"How would this matter be viewed, then, by the eye of the world, and what would be the opinion of it, when it comes to be related, that George Washington has received twenty thousand dollars and five thousand pounds sterling of the public money as an interest therein? Would not this, in the estimation of it, (if I am entitled to any merit for the part I have acted, and without it there is no foundation for the act), deprive me of the principal thing which is laudable in my conduct?"[1] In a subsequent letter to Patrick Henry, Harrison's successor as governor of Virginia, Washington speaks of his original determination to accept

[1] Pickell, p. 135, or Writings of Washington, IX., p. 84. Washington's private opinion as to the effect the Potomac enterprise would have in raising the value of his western lands, may be gathered from a comparison of his Writings, IX., pp. 81, 99.

no pay whatever for his public services: "When I was first called to the station with which I was honored during the late conflict for our liberties, to the diffidence which I had so many reasons to feel in accepting it, I thought it my duty to join a firm resolution to shut my hand against every pecuniary recompense. To this resolution I have invariably adhered, and from it, if I had the inclination, I do not feel at liberty now to depart "[1] But, in view of the earnest wishes of Patrick Henry and the legislature of Virginia, that Washington's name might be identified with this great scheme for public improvements, Washington finally consented to appropriate the shares, not to his own emolument, but for objects of a public nature.

The shares that Washington received from the Potomac Company seem to have constituted the material basis of his famous plan for a National University. An examination of his correspondence with Edmund Randolph and Thomas Jefferson, reveals the fact that Washington's original purpose was to appropriate the Potomac and James river stock for the establishment of two charity schools, one on each of the above rivers for the education and support of the children of those men who had fallen in the defence of American liberty.[2] Afterwards, however, believing the stock likely to prove extremely valuable, Washington determined to employ the fifty shares, which he held in the Potomac Company, for the endowment of a National University, in the District of Columbia, "under the auspices of the general government." The one hundred shares which he held in the James River Company, were given to Liberty Hall Academy, in Virginia, now the Washington and Lee University. Although Washington declared his conviction that it would be far better to concentrate all the shares upon the establishment of a National University,[3] yet, from a desire to reconcile his gratitude to Vir-

[1] Pickell, p. 143.
[2] Writings of Washington, IX., pp. 116, 134.
[3] Writings of Washington, XI., p. 24.

ginia with a great public good, he concluded to divide the bequest as above described. "I am disposed to believe," he writes to the governor and legislature of Virginia, "that a seminary of learning upon an enlarged plan, but yet not coming up to the full idea of a university, is an institution to be preferred for the position which is to be chosen. The students, who wish to pursue the whole range of science, may pass with advantage from the seminary to the University, and the former, by a due relation, may be rendered coöperative with the latter."[1]

The project of a National University was the favorite scheme of Washington's old age. It was more than an "enlarged plan;" it was a "full idea." In these days of striving for a broader knowledge of economic laws, for a better civil service, and for a thorough understanding of the principles of legislation, is it not well to consider for a moment Washington's plan for "the education of our youth in the science of government?" Since it is purely a matter of fact that the most trusty and efficient servants, of whom this country can boast, are trained at a governmental institution, which was suggested by George Washington in a speech to Congress, as second only to a National University, it is not unlikely that there may be some essence of political wisdom even in the latter project. Washington said "the art of war is at once comprehensive and complicated; it demands much previous study." The American people found out some years ago, that Washington was right on that point, and they are now beginning to suspect, that even the art of government requires some previous study, and that, possibly, "a flourishing state of the arts and sciences contributes to national prosperity and reputation."[2]

Washington's letters, after 1794, are full of allusions to his new scheme, and he never tires of expatiating upon the advantages which would arise from a school of politics where the future guar-

[1] Writings of Washington, XI., p. 24.
[2] Speech of Washington to Congress, December 7, 1796. Writings of Washington, XII., p. 71.

dians of liberty might receive their training. But there is a passage in Washington's last will and testament, which sums up his views upon this important matter: "It has always been a source of serious regret with me," he says, "to see the youth of these United States sent to foreign countries for the purpose of education, often before their minds were formed, or they had imbibed any adequate ideas of the happiness of their own; contracting, too frequently, not only habits of dissipation and extravagance, but *principles unfriendly to republican government*, ... which thereafter are rarely overcome; for these reasons it has been my ardent wish to see a plan devised, on a liberal scale, which would have a tendency to spread systematic ideas through all parts of this rising empire, thereby to do away with local attachments and State prejudices, as far as the nature of things would, or indeed ought to admit, from our national councils. Looking anxiously forward to the accomplishment of so desirable an object as this is, (in my estimation), my mind has not been able to contemplate any plan more likely to effect the measure, than the establishment of a university in the central part of the United States, to which the youths of fortune and talents from all parts thereof may be sent for the completion of their education in all branches of polite literature, in the arts and sciences, in acquiring knowledge in the principles of politics and good government." [1] . . . .

It was reserved for later times to see the establishment, not far from the borders of the Potomac, midway between North and South, and under the very shadow of Washington's monument, of an institution, which, if not national in name, is national, nay cosmopolitan, in spirit, and is striving to realize "the full idea of a university."

It remains now for us to point out the connecting links between the Past and Present, between the pioneer schemes of George

---

[1] Writings of Washington, I., p. 571. See also XI., p. 3.

Washington, for opening up communication with the Great West, and the railroad enterprise of to-day, which also is the outgrowth of public spirit, and not without its influence upon the development of this country or the permanent welfare of a republic of letters. The work of clearing the Potomac river from obstructions was never fully carried out, and only one dividend was ever paid upon the stock invested.[1] But the Chesapeake and Ohio Canal Company took up the enterprise and have achieved success. There is now perfect communication from tide-water to Cumberland, along the line of the Potomac, and Washington's scheme is thus far realized. According to a report made by the president of the Chesapeake and Ohio Canal Company, in 1851, this work is considered "as merely carrying out in a more perfect form the design of General Washington, and as naturally resulting from the views and measures originally suggested and advocated by him."[2]

But the true historic outcome of Washington's pioneer scheme must be sought for, not simply in the Chesapeake and Ohio Canal, which starting at Cumberland, brings down coal from the mountains to the sea, but in that "enlarged plan," which regards Cumberland, as Washington surely did, merely as a stepping-stone to intercourse with the Ohio Valley, the Great Lakes, and the Far West. It is interesting to note, that, when the hope of ever constructing a canal over the Alleghany mountains was given up, in 1826, in consequence of the report of the French engineers, who had been employed to survey the proposed routes, the Baltimore and Ohio railroad enterprise was undertaken, at the sugges-

---

[1] Report of the Chesapeake and Ohio Canal, 1851, p. 20. Washington had such confidence in the Potomac Company that he recommended his legatees to take each a share of the Potomac stock in his estate rather than the equivalent in money. He thought the income from tolls would be very large when navigation was once opened. The James River stock became productive in the course of a few years after Washington's death. Writings of Washington. Note by Sparks, XI., p. 4.

[2] Report on the Chesapeake and Ohio Canal, 1851, p. 20.

tion of Philip E. Thomas, who resigned his office as commissioner for Maryland in the Chesapeake and Ohio Canal project, and devoted himself, henceforth, to the task of winning back for Baltimore the line of western trade, which had been diverted from the Cumberland road by the Erie Canal, which was completed in 1825. In a report on this subject to the enterprising spirits of Baltimore, by Mr. Thomas, on the nineteenth of February, 1827, may be seen, not only the beginning of the first railroad enterprise in this country,[1] but also the revival of Washington's pioneer suggestions concerning the best route from the seaboard to the West. The following extract from this report has an historic significance which, has never been duly emphasized, or even placed in its proper connections: "Baltimore lies two hundred miles nearer to the navigable waters of the West than New York, and about one hundred miles nearer to them than Philadelphia: to which may be added the important fact, that the easiest, and by far the most practicable route through the ridge of mountains, which divide the Atlantic from the Western waters, *is along the depression formed by the Potomac in its passage through them.*"[2] Philip E. Thomas, a worthy successor of that enterprising spirit, Governor Johnson, of Maryland, who succeeded Washington as president of the Potomac Company, became the first president of the Baltimore and Ohio railroad. The legislature of Maryland voted the sum of $500,000, in 1828, for the encouragement of the work. This was the first legislative aid ever given in this country

---

[1] Three miles of tramway, constructed in 1827, from the granite quarries to the wharves at Quincy, Massachusetts, can hardly be called a *railroad enterprise*, any more than can the quarry tramways of England, which existed long before the opening of the first railroad in the world, from Manchester to Liverpool, in 1830, the same year as the opening of the Baltimore and Ohio, from this city to Ellicotts Mills, distant fourteen miles. A locomotive engine was, however, first used on the Quincy road, in 1829. The same was imported from England, where they were just coming into use upon quarry-tramways.

[2] History and Description of the Baltimore and Ohio Rail Road. By a Citizen of Baltimore. 1853. p. 12.

to railroad enterprise. An appropriation of $1,000,000 was afterwards recommended for it by committees in both houses of Congress, but the bill failed to pass, owing to the opposition of General Mercer,[1] president of the Chesapeake and Ohio Canal Company and chairman of the committee on roads and canals. But our Government detailed West Point graduates to aid in engineering this work, which has proved of truly national importance and a worthy outcome of the National Road. As this country is indebted to George Washington for the suggestion of both this work and of a military academy, where engineers are trained for the public service, it would seem as though, in one way or another, all lines of public policy lead us back to Washington, as all roads lead to Rome.

The connection of the Baltimore and Ohio with Washington's scheme for opening up the West to trade and commerce, cannot be disputed upon the ground that the application of steam revolutionized locomotion and the routes of travel. Steam had nothing whatever to do with the inception of the Baltimore and Ohio, for the first locomotive power employed on this road, the first division of which was opened in 1830, was horse-power. The Liverpool and Manchester road was opened the same year, and locomotive engines soon came into general use, but, on the Baltimore and Ohio, cars were first drawn, like canal boats, by horses and mules. The transitional character of this Baltimore enterprise is still further illustrated by the fact, that Evan Thomas rigged up a railway-car with sails, which was called the "Aeolus," and was pronounced a great success—on windy days. Baron Krudener, a Russian envoy to this country, about the time the experiment was made, was so delighted with the invention, that he said he would like to send over all his staff from Washington "to enjoy sailing on the railroad." The subsequent introduction of railways into Russia and the official patronage extended to Ross Winans, of

---

[1] History and Description of the Baltimore and Ohio Railroad, p. 22

Baltimore, for his mechanical inventions, are largely due to the glowing accounts of American enterprise given by Baron Krudener, after his return to St. Petersburg. But Ross Winans' invention of powerful locomotives and friction-wheels, did not originate the Baltimore and Ohio. They were the result of premiums offered to the inventive genius of America by Philip E. Thomas and his colleagues. The opening of a railroad, or of some better means of communication with the West than portage over the Cumberland road, became a living necessity for the merchants of Baltimore after the Erie Canal had turned the current of western trade. It was positively a struggle, for commercial existence. The construction of tramways, the use of horse power and of sails, and the final application of steam, and Ross Winans' inventions, were but a process of natural selection, and only the fittest has survived. But the historic germ of this wonderful evolution is Washington's pioneer scheme for opening up a channel of trade to the West by way of the Potomac. Of course external influence was necessary. The channels of enterprise must always be kept open, like the Suez Canal, by the constant effort of men.

The original idea of Washington concerning the Potomac route has become an "enlarged plan." *A road to the western waters* is the leading idea, from first to last, in the Reports of the Baltimore and Ohio railroad. This was the thought of Philip E. Thomas, and it is the thought to-day, for there are *still western waters*. The completion of "the great national route" to the Mississippi, was announced in 1857, and, in that year, occurred one of the greatest railway celebrations[1] this country has ever

---

[1] Book of Great Railway Celebrations in 1857. By William Prescott Smith. On pages 215-16 there is an interesting speech, delivered by Mr. George Bancroft, at the celebration in Cincinnati. His glowing tribute to Baltimore must not be forgotten: "This great work is emphatically the work of the City of Baltimore, and it may almost be said of Baltimore alone, for it was carried on without much favor from its own State, and sometimes in conflict with the rivalry of its neighbors. Nor is this all the marvel. The work in its completeness has cost more

witnessed, for three grand routes, the Baltimore and Ohio to Parkersburg, the Marietta and Cincinnati from Parkersburg, and the Ohio and Mississippi from Cincinnati to St. Louis, were simultaneously ended and formed into "a chain which can never be broken," as Washington once said of commercial enterprise between the East and West. The route which he suggested is now indeed "becoming the channel of the extensive and valuable trade of a rising empire "

By the waters of the Potomac, near our Nation's Capitol, there stands an unfinished monument, which, for the credit of this country, is sometimes said to symbolize the incompleteness of Washington's fame. All great facts in Washington's life are like an unfinished monument, if viewed in themselves alone, but the historic influence of great facts and grand ideas will flow on like the Potomac, ever widening in their course and deepening new channels continually. The river of trade, which Washington sought to open, has now become a vast flood of commercial enterprise, seeking a quick way to the sea past the Monumental City, which in art, science, and the encouragement of public good, is more truly grateful to Washington's memory than the city which bears his name.

than $31,000,000, and was entered upon with a brave heart and at a time when the real and personal property of Baltimore was less than $27,000,000. But Baltimore was always brave. In the gloomiest hour of the American Revolution, her voice of patriotism was loud and clear— her conduct an example to sister cities; and when has she been wanting to the cause of civil or religious freedom? . . . She is called the Monumental City. Her column rises as a memorial of the Father of his country; but this is her own monument. It spans the Alleghanies; it reaches from the waters of the Atlantic to the bosom of the Ohio. . . . . We celebrate the opening of the direct communication between Baltimore, Cincinnati, and St. Louis. The occasion is one of great national interest. The system of roads binds indissolubly together the East and the West. . . . . How would Washington have exulted, could he but have seen his great and cherished idea of an international highway carried out with a perfection and convenience which surpassed the power of his century to imagine!"

III.

THE MARYLAND INSTRUCTIONS.

"Instructions of the General Assembly of Maryland, to George Plater, William Paca, William Carmichael, John Henry, James Forbes, and Daniel of St. Thomas Jenifer, Esqrs:[1]

"GENTLEMEN, Having conferred upon you a trust of the highest nature, it is evident we place great confidence in your integrity, abilities and zeal to promote the general welfare of the United States, and the particular interest of this state, where the latter is not incompatible with the former; but to add greater weight to your proceedings in Congress, and to take away all suspicion that the opinions you there deliver, and the votes you give, may be the mere opinions of individuals, and not resulting from your knowledge of the sense and deliberate judgment of the state you represent, we think it our duty to instruct you as followeth on the subject of the confederation, a subject in which, unfortunately, a supposed difference of interest has produced an almost equal division of sentiments among the several states composing the union: We say a supposed difference of interests; for, if local attachments and prejudices, and the avarice and ambition of individuals, would give way to the dictates of a sound policy, founded on the principles of justice, (and no other policy but what is founded on those immutable principles deserves to be called sound,) we flatter ourselves this apparent diversity of interests would soon vanish; and all the states would confederate on terms mutually advantageous to all; for they would then perceive that no other confederation than one so formed can be lasting. Although the pressure of immediate calamities, the dread of their continuance from the appearance of disunion, and some other peculiar circumstances, may have induced some states to accede to the present

[1] See Journals of Congress, III., pp. 281-3.

confederation, contrary to their own interests and judgments, it requires no great share of foresight to predict, that when those causes cease to operate, the states which have thus acceded to the confederation will consider it as no longer binding, and will eagerly embrace the first occasion of asserting their just rights and securing their independence. Is it possible that those states, who are ambitiously grasping at territories, to which in our judgment they have not the least shadow of exclusive right, will use with greater moderation the increase of wealth and power derived from those territories, when acquired, than what they have displayed in their endeavours to acquire them? we think not; we are convinced the same spirit which hath prompted them to inlist on a claim so extravagant, so repugnant to every principle of justice, so incompatible with the general welfare of all the states, will urge them on to add oppression to injustice. If they should not be incited by a superiority of wealth and strength to oppress by open force their less wealthy and less powerful neighbours, yet the depopulation, and consequently the impoverishment of those states, will necessarily follow, which by an unfair construction of the confederation may be stripped of a common interest in, and the common benefits derivable from, the western country. Suppose, for instance, Virginia indisputably possessed of the extensive and fertile country to which she has set up a claim, what would be the probable consequences to Maryland of such an undisturbed and undisputed possession? they cannot escape the least discerning.

"Virginia, by selling on the most moderate terms a small proportion of the lands in question, would draw into her treasury vast sums of money, and in proportion to the sums arising from such sales, would be enabled to lessen her taxes: lands comparatively cheap and taxes comparatively low, with the lands and taxes of an adjacent state, would quickly drain the state thus disadvantageously circumstanced of its most useful inhabitants, its wealth; and its consequence in the scale of the confederated states would sink of course. A claim so injurious to more tha one-half, if not to the whole of the United States, ought to be supported by the clearest evidence of the right. Yet what evidences of that right have been produced? what arguments alleged in support either of the evidence or the right; none that we have heard of deserving a serious refutation.

"It has been said that some of the delegates of a neighbouring state have declared their opinion of the impracticability of governing the extensive dominion claimed by that state: hence also the necessity was admitted of dividing its territory and erecting a new state, under the auspices and direction of the elder, from whom no doubt it would receive its form of government, to whom it would be bound by some alliance or confederacy, and by whose councils it would be influenced: such a measure, if ever attempted, would certainly be opposed by the other states, as inconsistent with the letter and spirit of the proposed confederation. Should it take place, by establishing a sub-confederacy, *imperium in imperio*, the state possessed of this extensive dominion must then either submit to all the inconveniences of an overgrown and unwieldy government, or suffer the authority of Congress to interpose at a future time, and to lop off a part of its territory to be erected into a new and free state, and admitted into the confederation on such conditions as shall be settled by nine states. If it is necessary for the happiness and tranquillity of a state thus overgrown, that Congress should hereafter interfere and divide its territory; why is the claim to that territory now made and so pertinaciously insisted on? we can suggest to ourselves but two motives; either the declaration of relinquishing at some future period a portion of the country now contended for, was made to lull suspicion asleep, and to cover the designs of a secret ambition, or if the thought was seriously entertained, the lands are now claimed to reap an immediate profit from the sale. We are convinced policy and justice require that a country unsettled at the commencement of this war, claimed by the British crown, and ceded to it by the treaty of Paris, if wrested from the common enemy by the blood and treasure of the thirteen states, should be considered as a common property, subject to be parcelled out by Congress into free, convenient and independent governments, in such manner and at such times as the wisdom of that assembly shall hereafter direct. Thus convinced, we should betray the trust reposed in us by our constituents, were we to authorize you to ratify on their behalf the confederation, unless it be farther explained: we have coolly and dispassionately considered the subject; we have weighed probable inconveniences and hardships against the sacrifice of just and essential rights; and do instruct you not to agree to the confederation, unless an article or articles be added thereto in conformity with our declaration: should we succeed in obtaining such article or articles, then you are hereby fully empowered to accede to the confederation.

"That these our sentiments respecting the confederation may be more publicly known and more explicitly and concisely declared, we have drawn up the annexed declaration, which we instruct you to lay before Congress, to have it printed, and to deliver to each of the delegates of the other states in Congress assembled, copies thereof, signed by yourselves or by such of you as may be present at the time of the delivery; to the intent and purpose that the copies aforesaid may be communicated to our brethren of the United States, and the contents of the said declaration taken into their serious and candid consideration.

"Also we desire and instruct you to move at a proper time, that these instructions be read to Congress by their secretary, and entered on the journals of Congress.

"We have spoken with freedom, as becomes freemen, and we sincerely wish that these our representations may make such an impression on that assembly as to induce them to make such addition to the articles of confederation as may bring about a permanent union.

"A true copy from the proceedings of December 15, 1778.

Test, T. DUCKETT, C. H. D."

IV.

Maryland's Accession to the Confederation.

"An act to empower the Delegates of this State in Congress to subscribe and ratify the Articles of Confederation.[1]

"Whereas it hath been said that the common enemy is encouraged by this state not acceding to the confederation, to hope that the union of the sister states may be dissolved; and therefore prosecutes the war in expectation of an event so disgraceful to America; and our friends and illustrious ally are impressed with an idea that the common cause would be promoted by our formally acceding to the confederation: this general assembly, conscious that this state hath, from the commencement of the war, strenuously exerted herself in the common cause, and fully satisfied that if no formal confederation was to take place, it is the fixed determination of this state to continue her exertions to the utmost, agreeable to the faith pledged in the union; from an earnest desire to conciliate the affection of the sister states; to convince all the world of our unalterable resolution to support the independence of the United States, and the alliance with his most Christian majesty, and to destroy forever any apprehension of our friends, or hope in our enemies, of this state being again united to Great-Britain.

"Be it enacted by the general assembly of Maryland, that the delegates of this state in Congress, or any two or three of them, shall be, and are hereby, empowered and required, on behalf of this state, to subscribe the articles of confederation and perpetual union between the states of New-Hampshire, Massachusetts-Bay, Rhode-Island and Providence Plantations, Connecticut, New-York, New-Jersey, Pennsylvania, Delaware, Maryland, Virginia, North-Carolina, South-Carolina, and Georgia, signed in the gen-

---

[1] Journals of Congress, III., pp. 576–7.

eral Congress of the said states by the hon. Henry Laurens, esq. their then president, and laid before the legislature of this state to be ratified if approved. And that the said articles of confederation and perpetual union, so as aforesaid subscribed, shall henceforth be ratified and become conclusive as to this state, and obligatory thereon. And it is hereby declared, that, by acceding to the said confederation, this state doth not relinquish, or intend to relinquish, any right or interest she hath, with the other united or confederated states, to the back country; but claims the same as fully as was done by the legislature of this state, in their declaration, which stands entered on the journals of Congress; this state relying on the justice of the several states hereafter, as to the said claim made by this state.

"And it is further declared, that no article in the said confederation, can or ought to bind this or any other state, to guarantee any exclusive claim of any particular state, to the soil of the said back lands, or any such claim of jurisdiction over the said lands or the inhabitants thereof.

"By the House of Delegates, January 30th, 1781, read and assented to,   By order,   F. GREEN, *Clerk.*

"By the Senate, February 2d, 1781. Read and assented to.
    By order,   JAS. MACCUBBIN, *Clerk.*
THO. S. LEE.   (L. S.)"

V.

PELATIAH WEBSTER'S VIEWS ON OUR TERRITORIAL COMMONWEALTH IN 1781.

Pelatiah Webster was that "able though not conspicuous citizen," to whom Madison ascribes the credit of first publicly suggesting, that the Old Congress should call a Continental Convention, for the purpose of revising and enlarging congressional powers.[1] Curtis, in his History of the Constitution, after quoting Madison's statement concerning the pioneer character of Pelatiah Webster's pamphlet, published at the seat of Congress in May, 1781, simply remarks: "Recent researches have not added to our knowledge of this writer."[2] Curtis makes no mention of Pelatiah Webster's "Political Essays on the Nature and Operation of Money, Public Finances, and other subjects," published during the American War and collected in 1791. A copy of this somewhat rare book has recently come into the possession of the author, and is found to contain, among other valuable papers, an essay on the Western Lands, first published in Philadelphia, April 25, 1781, not quite a month, therefore, after Maryland's Accession to the Confederation. Pelatiah Webster's views upon the subject of our Territorial Commonwealth are so strikingly similar to the ideas originally advanced by Maryland, that they will be read with interest, and are deserving of profound respect, for Pelatiah Webster seems to have been, not only an American type of Adam Smith, in questions of political economy, but a power behind the scenes, in Philadelphia, the seat of the old Congress. In an essay, by Noah Webster, on the Origin of the Bank, Pelatiah Webster is spoken of as "an old, intelligent merchant of Philadelphia, whose practical knowledge of money concerns gave him great influence, and whose opinions were often consulted by the gentlemen of Congress."[3]

Noah Webster, according to Madison, was one of the first to suggest a national government acting upon individuals; and it may yet appear that Pelatiah Webster had some hand in the intellectual frame-work of our Constitution, for his dissertation on the Political Union and Constitution of the Thirteen United

[1] Madison Papers, pp. 706-7. See also Note 172 by Madison's editor.
[2] History of the Constitution of the United States, I., p 351.
[3] Collection of Papers on Political, Literary, and Moral Subjects. By Noah Webster. New York, 1843, p. 163.

States of North America, first published at Philadelphia, in 1783, must, at that time, have exercised considerable influence, and it is not altogether without suggestive ideas, even for modern political reformers.

The following brief selections from Pelatiah Webster's essay on Western Lands[1] will serve to indicate its scope and tenor: "The whole territory or extent of the Thirteen States is the aggregate of them all, i. e., the territory or extent of each of the States added together, make the whole territory or extent of right and dominion of the United States; and, of course, whatever is comprehended within the boundaries of each State, now makes a part of our Commonwealth. This is to be considered as our present possession, our present decided right, which is guarantied to us by the treaty with France (Article XI.) together with 'any additions or conquests, which our Confederation may obtain during the war from any of the dominions now or heretofore possessed by Great Britain in North America.' . . . .

"It is further to be noted here, that with respect to *Virginia*, and some other governments, which either never had any charters, or whose charters have been surrendered to the crown, that the *soil and jurisdiction* of them were *both in the crown*, and therefore the King *ever* claimed the right to make new grants of soil, and carve out and establish any new jurisdictions or governments which he thought expedient, and on this principle actually did carve *Maryland* and part of *Pennsylvania* out of *Virginia ;* how justly I am not to say; but this does not hinder Virginia from taking her departure from her eastern boundary on the sea-coast, and covering all the lands within her limits (not included in these *carvatures*) to her utmost western boundary.

[1] The exact title of this essay is " The Extent and Value of our Western unlocated Lands and the proper Method of disposing of them, so as to gain the greatest possible Advantage from them " It must be classed with Thomas Paine's Public Good (1780) and with Plain Facts (1781) as constituting the chief pamphlet-literature, relating to the land controversy.

"It is, indeed, to be observed here, that ascertaining the boundaries of any State, does not prove the *title or right of such State to all lands* included within such boundaries. There is a distinction to be made between those lands which have been *alienated by the crown*, the title of which, at the date of our independence, was not in the crown, but vested in particular persons, either sole or aggregate, and those which *remained in the crown*, the title of which the crown then held in right of its sovereignty, which was a right vested in the supreme authority, in nature of a trust for the use of the public.

"There is no doubt but every right and title of all persons and bodies politic are as effectually secured and confirmed to the owners, to all intents and purposes, under the *Commonwealth*, as they were formerly *under the crown;* but it cannot be admitted that any individual or bodies politic should acquire *new rights* by the Revolution, to which they were not entitled under the crown. . . . . . .

"Indeed, in all revolutions of government which have ever happened in Europe, and, perhaps, in the whole world, all *crownlands, jewels,* and *all other estate* which belonged to the supreme power which *lost* the government, ever passed by the revolution into the supreme power which *gained* it. . . . . .

"Nor can I see the least pretence of reason, why we should depart from a rule of right grounded on the most plain and natural fitness, adopted by every nation in the world under like circumstances, and justified and confirmed by the experience and sanction of ages. I think that nothing but our unacquaintedness with the heights to which we are risen, the high sphere in which we now move, and an incapacity of viewing and judging of things on a great scale, could give rise to so extravagant an idea, as that *one State* should be *more entitled than another* to the crownlands, or any other property of the crown, which ever was in its nature public, and ought to continue so, or be disposed of for the use and benefit of the whole public community; or that one State should acquire more right, or property, or estate than another, by that Revolution which was the *joint act*, procured and perfected by the *joint effort* and *expense* of the whole. We have too long and too ridiculously set up to be wiser than all the world besides, and too long refused to be instructed by the experience of other nations."[1]

---

[1] Political Essays by Pelatiah Webster. Philadelphia, 1791, pp. 485-90.

TABLE TO APPENDIX.

		PAGE.
I.	Washington's Land Speculations,	72
II.	Washington's Public Spirit in Opening a Channel of Trade between East and West,	92
III.	The Maryland Instructions,	114
IV.	Maryland's Accession to the Confederation,	118
V.	Pelatiah Webster's Views on National Commonwealth,	119

www.ingramcontent.com/pod-product-compliance
Lightning Source LLC
Chambersburg PA
CBHW021940160426
43195CB00011B/1173